Praise for *God: T*

"This book is at the same time a pe
spiritual odyssey and an informative overview or the
relationship between religion and science. It will challenge
believers and nonbelievers."
   —**Hans Küng**

"Patrick Glynn has written a thoughtful and provocative
book about new scientific evidence for the existence of
God and the inability of rationalism to deal with
ultimate questions."
   —**Robert H. Bork**

"Elegantly written and absorbing."
   —***National Review***

"Argues persuasively that science, once a crutch for those
who would deny God, in the next century will be a force
for moving those with eyes to see and ears to hear in the
other direction."
   —***Orange County Register***

"This thoughtful and documented book may help more
intellectuals to understand that humans searching for
evidence of God is much like a wave on an ocean searching
for evidence that the ocean exists."
   —**Sir John M. Templeton,** founder of the Templeton Prize for
Progress in Religion and author of
The Humble Approach:Scientists Discover God

"Patrick Glynn has scouted the terrain of what may be the
most exciting cultural event of the twenty-first century.
The new dialogue between scientists and religious believers,
made possible by both theological advances and the
incredibility of fundamentalist naturalism, can't come too
soon—it's only about 400 years overdue. Kudos to Glynn
for helping to move the conversation into high gear."
   —**George Weigel,** senior fellow, Ethics and Public Policy Center

GOD
The Evidence

The Reconciliation of Faith and

Reason in a Postsecular World

PATRICK GLYNN

THREE RIVERS PRESS

NEW YORK

For my mother, Kathleen Glynn

Published by Three Rivers Press, New York, New York. Member of the Crown Publishing Group, a division of Random House, Inc.
www.crownpublishing.com

THREE RIVERS PRESS and the Tugboat design are registered trademarks of Random House, Inc.

Originally published by Prima Publishing, Roseville, California, in 1999.

Printed in the United States of America

Library of Congress Cataloging-in-Publication Data

Glynn, Patrick.
God : the evidence : the reconciliation of faith and reason in a postsecular world.
p. cm.
Includes bibliographical references and index.
ISBN 0-7615-1964-5
1. God—Proof, Cosmological.   2. Anthropic principle.   3. Natural theology.
4. Religion and science.   I. Title.
8T102.G575   1997
212'.1—dc21   97-18354
                                                              CIP

10 9 8 7

First Paperback Edition

Contents

ACKNOWLEDGMENTS   vii

introduction
The Making and Unmaking of an Atheist   1

one
A Not-So-Random Universe   21

two
Psyche and Soul:
Postsecularism in Psychology   57

three
Faith and the Physicians   79

four
Intimations of Immortality   99

five
Reason and Spirit   139

NOTES   171

INDEX   201

Acknowledgments

When my wife, Gabriele, and I first met, she would make occasional use of the word "spiritual." At the time I had no clear idea what she meant; I thought the spiritual was merely a product of the human imagination. Today I know better. From the beginning, our life together has been an intellectual and spiritual collaboration. That is no less true of this book. Gabriele lived through every step of it, and without her it simply would not have been written. She was a sounding board and a source of ideas, the critical but supportive reader of every draft. We talked through every stage of the argument together. The text is peppered with her editorial suggestions and substantive insights. She always knew when my writing was "on" and had a very nice way of letting me know when it wasn't. Gabriele was also constantly supportive in other ways—uncomplaining when I was forced to spend the better part of a Saturday and Sunday in front of the computer, or when my mood became glum and preoccupied because a particular section was giving me trouble. No author could ask for a more generous, loving, or intelligent partner. I love her. I thank God every day for sending her to me.

Steven Martin of Prima Publishing wrote to me after reading a short piece I wrote on cosmology and the God question for *National Review*. His belief in the possibility of this book helped to make it a reality. The Prima editorial team, including senior editor Betsy Towner Levine, was the picture of competence and a pleasure to work with from start to finish.

George Weigel, then president and now senior fellow at the Ethics and Public Policy Center, provided through his organization the 501C-3 "umbrella" for a small grant that enabled me to bridge into the project after leaving the American Enterprise Institute. Both George and his successor as president of the center, Elliot Abrams, were supportive of the project proposal, and I am appreciative.

When my writing on politics and public policy began to take a "spiritual" turn a couple of years ago, Amitai Etzioni was one of the first people in Washington to notice the change and one of the few to respond wholly positively. In February 1997, Amitai raised the possibility of my joining his Communitarian research center at George Washington University. His friend and supporter Norton Garfinkle, now chairman of the George Washington University Institute for Communitarian Policy Studies, provided the wherewithal to create the position of associate director of the institute and permitted me to work at the job part-time until *God: The Evidence* was complete. It was a key to finishing the book, and I am grateful to both of them.

Finally, in my stepson, Kai Hills, I have had all the advantages of a son, with none of the usual work that goes into fatherhood. He was kind enough to read the introduction to the book in manuscript form and—much to my delight—said he liked it. I hope other readers feel the same.

The Making
and Unmaking
of an Atheist

This book had its origins in a spiritual awakening—
or, to put the situation somewhat less glamorously,
after many years of being a philosophical atheist or agnostic, I finally realized that there was in fact a God. A God, a
soul, a survival after death. This, of course, would not be news
to most people. Depending on how you interpret opinion
polls, upwards of 70 percent of Americans seem to share
such beliefs.[1] But for me, as I think would be true for many
others like me, and possibly even for some of you, it *was* news.
Big news.

For despite the fact that the overwhelming majority of
Americans are believers, our intellectual culture has been dominated by skepticism. When I did undergraduate and graduate

work at Harvard in the 1970s, for example, it was taken for granted that traditional religious beliefs were a thing of the past, invalidated by science, incompatible with a modern outlook. There were believers among the professors, of course. But the culture was agnostic. There was a certain tendency, which I came to share, to view religious belief and practice as manifestations of intellectual inconsistency, emotional weakness, or a lack of cultural sophistication.

This is an old complaint among religiously minded people, and I don't wish to add my voice to those of the complainers. I would argue instead—and I try to show in this book—that the situation is in the process of changing. The day, I believe, is soon coming when skepticism, unbelief, is going to be the minority position, not just among the populace at large, but even among intellectuals. What happened to me—the rediscovery of the spiritual—is happening to others and is on the verge of happening to our culture as a whole.

The reason lies in a series of dramatic new developments in science, medicine, and other fields that have radically transformed the old existence-of-God debate. Essentially, over the past twenty years, a significant body of evidence has emerged, shattering the foundations of the long-dominant modern secular worldview. These new discoveries, it seems to me, add up to a powerful—indeed, all-but-incontestable—case for what once was considered a completely debatable matter of "faith": the existence of soul, afterlife, and God.

I came upon these new discoveries rather late in the game—long after I had decided, on the basis of intensive philosophical study, that there was no God in a personal sense, no afterlife, no soul. I embraced skepticism at an early age, when I first learned of Darwin's theory of evolution in, of all places, Catholic grade school. It immediately occurred to me that either Darwin's theory was true or the creation story in the Book of Genesis was true. They could not both be true, and I stood up in class and told the poor nun as much.

Thus began a long odyssey away from the devout religious belief and practice that had marked my childhood toward an increasingly secular and rationalistic outlook. I was not alone on this journey. In the 1960s, American culture was entering a secular phase. Vatican Council II—the great leap of the Catholic Church into modernity—had left even devout Catholics with many questions about their faith. The period was rife with exper-imental notions, and religious intellectuals were increasingly ab-sorbing the secular themes and tendencies of the larger culture. In 1965, theologian Harvey Cox published *The Secular City*, an enormously influential book that argued that the churches should simply abandon all notions of transcendence and spirit in favor of a new model of positive social change based on secular social science.[2] The following year, *Time* magazine, surveying the state of contemporary theology, asked on its cover "Is God Dead?"[3]

In the universities, He *was* dead, or appeared to be. When I left my Jesuit high school to attend Harvard in 1969, I plunged into an environment where the death or disappearance of God was simply taken for granted. In those days, the era of "New Left" ascendancy and anti–Vietnam War protests, the curricu-lum was dominated by the writings of the atheist Karl Marx, whose work had assumed an importance that professors of an earlier age might have granted only to the Bible. Even in my department, English—which was largely free of political and Marxist tendencies—the emphasis of the curriculum was on secular themes. English at Harvard was really a course in intellectual history, and Western intellectual history seemed to be the story of what Yale literary scholar J. Hillis Miller called "the disappearance of God":[4] the gradual loss of faith by the novelists, poets, and great thinkers of the West.

It was not so much that the professors who taught me were antireligious—the English department faculty (apart from a couple of practicing Catholics and a few other churchgoers) was marked by a kind of sad yearning for lost Christianity. It was simply assumed that religious belief had become impossible for rational human beings in the modern era, a fact that one accepted with a certain melancholy and nostalgia for previous ages when it was still possible for "men" to believe. Some thought, following the nineteenth-century writer Matthew Arnold, that with religion gone, literature would somehow have to take its place. But this was a halfhearted notion.

Such views reflected the confidence of the intellectual world that modern science had destroyed all rational foundation for the religious worldview. "We moderns" were the heirs of the two great scientific revolutions: the Copernican and the Darwinian. Copernicus had shown that, contrary to the suggestion of the Bible, humanity was in no sense at the "center" of the cosmos. The earth was merely one planet orbiting the sun, which, in turn, as modern astronomy gradually discovered, was merely one of billions of stars in a universe billions of light-years across. Moreover, Darwin had demonstrated that it was not even necessary to posit a God to explain the origin of life. Life, and the human species itself, was the outcome of essentially random mechanisms operating over the eons. The creation story set forth in the Book of Genesis merely reflected the ignorance and naïveté of our ancestors, who had invented the idea of God as a kind of defense mechanism to help them cope with the rigors of survival. Humanity was not God's creation; rather, we were, as the atheistic philosopher and mathematician Bertrand Russell once put it, "a curious accident in a backwater,"[5] the inexplicable by-product of what was often referred to, in those days, as the "random universe."

By the time I graduated from Harvard, I had thoroughly absorbed this modern, secular viewpoint. But I remained a genuine "agnostic." I thought the existence of God very, very unlikely, but I did not know. So, after a year at Cambridge University on a fellowship, I returned to graduate school at Harvard to plumb the depths of Western philosophy. By the time I received my Ph.D. at the end of the 1970s, I was a convinced atheist.

The embrace of atheism did not bring joy. Somewhere, despite my "agnosticism," I had clung to the hope that I might be proven wrong. The day I grasped that the entire tradition of Western philosophy, from ancient to modern times, was essentially a refutation of the religious worldview—of the idea of God—was not a happy one. But the conclusion seemed inescapable. Reason, I thought, was the only path to truth. Reason could know only the following: that there was some intelligence or coherence to the nature of things that made reasoning, and for that matter science, possible; that human beings had a yearning for the divine; that public morality was necessary to maintain the social order. The yearnings for God, for a life after death, for justice in the universe, were just that: yearnings, wishes, with no basis in fact. The notion that God or "the gods" somehow reward virtue and punish wrongdoing was common to all human societies. But human societies defined virtue and wrongdoing in vastly different ways. They also had widely varying notions of God or "the gods." All these were fictions, human "conventions," that human beings, in their ignorance, had mistaken for nature, for reality.

Nearly all the great philosophers had recognized this, even the philosophers whom the Christian world had mistaken for monotheists: Socrates and Plato. Socrates debates the existence of the afterlife on his deathbed in Plato's *Phaedo* because he is not prepared to believe it. Hamlet debates the existence of an afterlife when he contemplates suicide because Shakespeare had the same skeptical view of such human beliefs as Socrates (Shakespeare was a writer in the Platonic tradition). The difference between ancient and modern philosophy essentially came down to an issue of discretion: The ancient philosophers attempted to conceal their atheism, while the modern philosophers broadcast their atheism from the housetops. The ancients were more discreet partly because the stakes were higher: In the old days, you could be persecuted and even executed for heterodox beliefs—witness the death of Socrates. But the ancient philosophers also felt that promoting atheism publicly would ultimately endanger the philosopher himself, since it would render society immoral and anarchic. Socrates learned this lesson firsthand when a number of students in whom he inculcated his atheistic views turned out to be a menace to Athenian society.[6]

So there it was. Not a pretty truth. In fact, I thought, an ugly one. But truth nonetheless. No God in the personal sense, no afterlife, no soul, no inherent justice in the universe. We were on our own.

Ironically, at the very time I was plumbing the depths of philosophical nihilism, science itself, unbeknownst to me and to many other people, was taking a surprising new turn. In 1973, in a lecture to the International Astronomical Union in Poland, the physicist and cosmologist Brandon Carter called attention to something he called "the anthropic principle." The anthropic principle, as Western thinkers are only now beginning to understand, amounted to a refutation of the original premise of the overarching modern philosophical idea: that of the "random universe."

All of us intellectuals had been proceeding on the assumption that our appearance in the universe had been entirely accidental, a random outcome of collisions of matter and of the eons-long process of evolution. It turned out that the picture was not so simple. In the hundred years and more since Darwin first proposed evolution by natural selection, scientists' understanding of the nature of the universe had greatly broadened and deepened. Using insights from relativity and particle physics in combination with observations from astronomy, modern cosmologists had been able to go a long way toward reconstructing the evolution of the entire universe, from its origins in the big bang.

The implications of this bigger picture were quite different from those that people had inferred from Darwin's theory. Suddenly, the universe, and human life, did not look so "random" or accidental after all. As Carter pointed out (in an unfortunately technical and roundabout way), life had to be, in effect, "pre-planned" from the very origin of the cosmos. In order to get life to appear in the universe billions of years after the universe began, you had to start planning very early—from the first nanosecond of the universe's coming into being. The possibility of producing life depended on everything's being "just right" from the very start—everything from the values of fundamental forces like electromagnetism and gravity, to the relative masses of the various subatomic particles, to things like the number of neutrino types at time 1 second, which the universe has to "know" already at 10^{-43} second. The slightest tinkering with a single one of scores of basic values and relationships in nature would have resulted in a universe very different from the one we inhabit—say, one with no stars like our sun, or no stars, period. Far from being accidental, life appeared to be the goal toward which the entire universe from the very first moment of its existence had been orchestrated, fine-tuned.

Secular-minded scientists have not been happy with this discovery, for it seems to go one step short of suggesting that the universe is "designed" for life. Indeed, today the case for design looks very strong. Dissatisfied with such an implication, scientists have proposed numerous counter-hypotheses. For example, some scientists have speculated that there may exist billions of "parallel" universes—which, mind you, we will never be able to detect—of which ours just happens to be one. If there were billions of invisible universes, then the series of miraculous coincidences that produced life in this one might not seem so unlikely. One hears a great deal about "other" universes in cosmology today: "parallel universes," "baby universes," "bubble universes." But these appeals to invisible universes have a certain unpersuasive quality to them: They are reminiscent of medieval theologians' speculations about the number of angels that could dance on the head of a pin.

The anthropic principle marked an important turning point in the history of science: the first time a scientific discovery seemed to take us toward, rather than away from, the idea that there is a God. For hundreds of years science had been whittling away at the proposition that the universe was created or designed. Suddenly, scientists came upon a series of facts that seemed to point toward precisely such a conclusion—that the universe is the product of intelligence and aim, that in the absence of intelligent organization of a thousand details vast and small, we would not exist.

Two years later came another discovery, far afield from the realm of astronomy and physics. Raymond Moody, a psychiatrist, published a book called *Life After Life,* recounting what he called "near-death experiences," deathbed visions of people who had "died and made a comeback." Such people, victims of serious accidents, heart attacks, or other near-death crises, brought back detailed descriptions of what they called a realm beyond death. They described leaving their bodies and witnessing medical resuscitation procedures from a point above the operating table. They told of having a sudden sense of peace and detachment, an absence of pain. Some described moving through a "tunnel" to a heavenly landscape with vivid colors and encountering a "Being of Light" that emanated a powerful, unearthly love. Many identified this Being as Christ. Some reported being greeted by relatives who had passed away. A few actually recounted undergoing a detailed "review" of their lives—a three-dimensional sequential replay of every thought, action, feeling, and event they had lived through, as well as the reactions of the people they interacted with—during which the Being offered a critical commentary and in which they felt joy, shame, humiliation, or sorrow, depending on whether they had done right or wrong. Those who had such "near-death experiences" insisted that they were real, not hallucinatory. Many claimed the experience had changed their lives.

Initially, the scientific community was prepared to dismiss these experiences out of hand as so many hallucinations. Even today many scientists—for the most part, those unfamiliar with the detailed research in the area—still assume such an explanation to be adequate. But a small army of trained researchers following in Moody's footsteps have corroborated his initial findings, and several researchers have produced compelling evidence—that is, closely documented cases of "autoscopic" perception—suggesting that so-called out-of-body experiences do occur. The majority of researchers who have investigated the phenomenon, generally professionals with medical, psychological, or other scientific training—many of whom started out as skeptics—have concluded that these experiences are authentic.

If the anthropic principle represented a rediscovery of order—and seemingly of design—in the universe, then near-death research offered the first systematic body of evidence suggestive of the existence of a soul.

The 1970s were a period of intellectual ferment, and other developments followed. One of the most important transformations took place in the field of psychiatry and psychology. Since the days of Sigmund Freud, psychiatry and psychology had been bastions of atheism. (At one point, no more than 1.1 percent of the membership of the American Psychological Association reported having any form of belief in God—in contrast with the 95 percent of the American population who claimed to accept the existence of some sort of Supreme Being.)[7] Freud, of course, had characterized religious belief not only as an "illusion," but also as a "neurosis"—in effect, a collective mental disorder that humanity was in the process of outgrowing. Yet beginning in the 1970s, evidence began to emerge showing a powerful correlation between religious commitment and overall mental health. A few mental health professionals began to insist on the necessity of factoring "spiritual" considerations into therapy. Most notable was psychiatrist M. Scott Peck, whose 1978 book, *The Road Less Traveled: A New Psychology of Love, Traditional Values, and Spiritual Growth,* spurred a virtual revolution in thinking about therapy. Peck criticized the psychiatric profession for ignoring and denigrating religious belief and argued that mental health could not be separated from considerations of spiritual belief and morality. His book rocketed to the *New York Times* best-seller list, where it remained for more than ten years. By the 1980s an increasing number of physicians and researchers were probing the so-called mind-body connection and the apparent link between religious or spiritual commitment and physical health. Today there is growing evidence that *physical* health, too, may have a spiritual dimension.

Not until the early 1990s did I become aware of these revolutionary developments, beginning with the literature on near-death experiences. Because I had surveyed the evidence relating to the existence of God so carefully in the 1970s (though still unaware of near-death research and the as yet little-known anthropic principle), I could see immediately how radically the intellectual landscape had changed. The totality of the evidence as I understood it in the mid-1970s suggested one conclusion. Today the evidence suggests quite a different one.

I am not claiming that anyone today can reason his or her way to faith in God. This was not even true in my case. For one thing, there was a stage in my life when I never would have bothered to pick up or read a book on near-death experiences, simply because such literature did not fit with my preconceptions of what was important or what was true. (Indeed, I came across a magazine article on one such experience in the 1980s. I read it, was puzzled, and then dismissed it from my mind. I thought I already knew the truth.)

St. Paul writes that faith is a "gift" of God.[8] My own experience supports this. Two things were necessary, I believe, before I was able to open my mind sufficiently even to notice the new evidence. One was a decision that I made, and the other was an encounter that was given to me.

The decision that I made was to reject nihilism as a basis for moral decision-making. It took me many years to arrive at this point, and I did so only after finding through experience that a nihilistic outlook was existentially unsustainable. For years I had gone along accepting the "solution" to nihilism proposed by the twentieth-century German Jewish émigré philosopher Leo Strauss. Strauss, a probing scholar of almost Talmudic meticulousness, had rediscovered the "esoteric" atheistic themes of the classical Greek philosophers but at the same time had recovered the rationale for their "esotericism" or secretiveness.[9] Strauss had witnessed the disastrous social and political consequences of the modern death-of-God philosophies. He had watched as Friedrich Nietzsche's idea of the "superman"—and the latter's celebration of the "noble virtues" of barbarism and cruelty—became the theme of German politics under Hitler. He had seen the man he always regarded as Nietzsche's rightful successor and Germany's most brilliant twentieth-century philosopher, Martin Heidegger, enthusiastically embrace the Nazi regime, with its viciously anti-Semitic policies. As a Jew, Strauss was no longer welcome in the German universities. Like so many other German Jewish intellectuals, he was in exile from Germany by the 1930s, first in Britain, and later America, where he contrived to found his own philosophical movement, based on the insights he had derived from the Platonic tradition.

The point of his work was this: The philosopher who discovered that there was no God and that all values were relative did not want to broadcast this insight to the populace at large. It was important to sustain a decent social order, even if the philosopher, in some sense, held in contempt the naïve beliefs on which the social order was based. The goal of life was to preserve the philosopher's freedom of inquiry—and, at some level, to save one's skin. Modern liberal democracy, whatever it lacked in "nobility," permitted this: It provided both freedom and a stable social order. Strauss became a privately atheistic, aristocratically minded, and conservative defender of liberal democracy—in particular against the surviving form of totalitarianism, Communism—and encouraged his students to do the same.[10] For many years, I made this cause my own—as a political journalist and later as an official of the Reagan administration. The byword of this way of life was "honor," essentially the sort of morality that Aristotle sets forth in his *Nichomachean Ethics*. But it was "skin-deep" morality, for at some level one had the secret atheist insight: If God is dead, then everything is permitted.[11]

Under such conditions, one's intentions may be generally good. But if you come to imagine that there is no moral order to the universe, the incentives to good conduct, particularly in private life, are, unfortunately, much weakened. There is little to justify great self-sacrifice or deep personal commitment. Indeed, it is hard, as I later saw in retrospect, to feel or express love to the fullest extent. Even if one cares for others and thinks one cares greatly, one is inclined to be guided in the final analysis by one's selfish wishes. What is there in the nihilist's universe to call forth sacrifice? And without a willingness to sacrifice, one's capacity to care for others is narrowly circumscribed. Such was my state in the early 1990s, when, rather than work on a marriage much in need of repair—and badly strained by my uncompromising commitment to my own intellectual and political projects—I sought a divorce, amicably, as the saying goes, more or less decently, but still with very painful consequences for my first wife and me.

The best explanation of this state of being I found much later in the work of a contemporary of Leo Strauss's, another Jewish exile from Nazi Germany, Martin Buber, who nonetheless, in my opinion, came much closer to true wisdom, partly because he did not suppose wisdom and goodness to be separate. Buber speaks of two "basic words" in which the life of a human being inheres: "I-It" and "I-You." It does not matter, as Buber points out, if the It is replaced by a He or a She.[12] The world of I-It is the world of utility, of using, of means and ends. It is a world of measurement and of comparison. The world of I-You is fundamentally different. It is the world of what Buber calls "encounter." When an I truly encounters a You—and this can be anyone from the love of one's life to a panhandler one meets on the street—measurement and comparison disappear. The You, when truly encountered, is immeasurable and directs us back to the Immeasurable.

Yet the encounter with the You requires a certain vulnerability, a willingness to risk the unpredictable possibilities of encounter, and ultimately a willingness to sacrifice. "It is up to you," Buber writes, "how much of the immeasurable becomes reality for you."[13] In embracing reason as my idol, I had turned my back on everything immeasurable and with it on the entire realm of I-You. I had submersed myself in a world where, in the final analysis, there was only I-It. The problem with the I-It world is that in it the I itself becomes "deactualized," as Buber notes.[14] It almost ceases to exist: "When man lets it have its way, the relentlessly growing It-world grows over him like weeds, his own I loses its actuality, until the incubus over him and the phantom inside him exchange the whispered confession of their need for redemption."[15]

Such was my condition when one afternoon in the early 1990s, with my Cold War "cause" and my marriage behind me, I made a decision. I decided that whatever I had done in the past, I now resolved to live honorably. Without exception. In small things and large. In the most private matters as well as the public ones. It was not that I believed in a God or an afterlife. I did not. I merely had come to see honor and conscience as a psychological necessity, as the sine qua non of a stable identity. If you did not adhere to your conscience, if there was nothing that in some way absolutely limited your conduct in life, then who were you, I asked myself? What were you?

In my mind was a fragmentary insight from an old column by George F. Will, commenting on Robert Bolt's superb play *A Man for All Seasons,* about the great English statesman and saint Sir Thomas More. Sir Thomas, Will wrote, had accepted death at the hands of Henry VIII rather than compromise his conscience and thereby his very identity.[16] This seemed to me a sound psychological insight. I opened my copy of Bartlett's to a passage I remembered from Winston Churchill. The quotation came from Churchill's tribute to his defeated political opponent, Neville Chamberlain, on the floor of the House of Commons in 1940. I began to commit the quotation, word by word, to memory:

> The only guide to a man is his conscience; the only shield to his memory is the rectitude and sincerity of his actions. It is very imprudent to walk through life without this shield, because we are so often mocked by the failure of our hopes and the upsetting of our calculations; but with this shield, however the fates may play, we march always in the ranks of honor.

I still regard this passage as the most concise, coherent, and persuasive argument for a strictly honorable life on purely secular grounds.

The first step, the rejection of nihilism, prepared me for the second—an encounter with love sufficiently deep to bring an intimation of the divine. It was shortly after my decision that I encountered Gabriele. Someone once said that it is hard to fall in love without thinking of God. Such was my experience. Ours was a wonderful romance that would culminate in marriage two years later. But these romantic feelings pointed me toward something deeper. I read much later Buber's notion that every true encounter with the You points to the You of God: "Extended, the lines of relationships intersect in the eternal You. Every single You is a glimpse of that. Through every single You the basic word addresses the eternal You."[17] Such was my experience, though I had no words to describe it. Beneath the feelings was something else. Buber writes:

Feelings accompany the metaphysical and metapsychical fact of love, but they do not constitute it; and the feelings that accompany it can be very different. Jesus' feeling for the possessed man is different from his feeling for the beloved disciple; but the love is one. Feelings one "has"; love occurs. Feelings dwell in man, but man dwells in his love. This is no metaphor but actuality: love does not cling to an I, as if the You were merely its "content" or object; it is between I and You. Whoever does not know this, know this with his being, does not know love, even if he should ascribe to it the feelings that he lives through, experiences, enjoys, and expresses. Love is a cosmic force. . . . Love is the responsibility of an I for a You: in this consists what cannot consist in any feeling—the equality of all lovers, from the smallest to the greatest and from the blissfully secure whose life is circumscribed by the life of one beloved human being to him that is nailed his life long to the cross of the world, capable of what is immense and bold enough to risk it: to love *man*.[18]

For reasons that I hardly understood, I began to utter from time to time a little prayer of thanksgiving.

I had not changed my mind. Gabriele was a believer, not a churchgoer at the time, but a strong spiritual Christian. And we debated the issue of God extensively—along with politics, psychology, foreign policy, and a dozen other topics. But I was not prepared to budge from a philosophical position that I had worked so hard to attain—even if my conduct was strangely parting ways with my philosophical framework. What happened, however, is that my mind became sufficiently open so that when, by happenstance, during our second summer together I came across a book on the afterlife in Crown Books, I picked it up and read it—first with interest and then with the dawning and somewhat horrifying realization that I had been wrong, wrong about everything, for upwards of twenty years.

Soon I worked my way through virtually the entire literature of near-death experiences—books by Raymond Moody, Elisabeth Kübler-Ross, and Melvin Morse. Eventually I spent several weeks in the National Library of Medicine in Bethesda, Maryland, poring over the scientific journals in which the more technical aspects of near-death research are explored and debated. I examined the arguments attempting to attribute near-death experiences to some form of hallucination, and I examined the analyses refuting these theories in turn. The evidence seemed to me overwhelmingly on the side of the nonskeptics.

Later I turned to the physical sciences and discovered that in the two or three decades since I had been introduced to the random, materialistic universe that is still the staple of modern education, this too had effectively been refuted or overtaken by an entirely new vision. I learned of the anthropic principle in cosmology and of the profound new mysteries of the cosmos that science had unearthed and could no longer adequately explain. It was clear that the old materialistic paradigm, the fundamental modern framework of the random, mechanistic universe, on which we proud intellectuals had based all our atheism and anxiety, was coming apart at the seams.

I broadened my search to psychology and medicine, and found parallel developments there.

Rapidly a picture emerged of a universe entirely different from the one I thought I had been living in. Gradually, I realized that in the twenty years since I opted for philosophical atheism, a vast, systematic literature had emerged that not only cast deep doubt on, but also, from any reasonable perspective, effectively refuted my atheistic outlook.

It was not just an intellectual realization. The discovery that I had been so dead wrong about the fundamentals of life sent me, I have to admit, into a bit of a psychological tailspin. I realized how wrong I had been, how selfish, how arrogant—I will say it—how sinful. It took time, reading, contemplation, reasoning, prayer, and a great deal of extremely patient help (and good humor) from Gabriele for me to work my way out of my spiritual froth back to an even keel, to determine what I did and did not believe about the nature of the spiritual universe, and to understand the limits of what indeed we could know about such things. But there were also spiritual experiences along the way—beckonings, intuitions, and even minor miracles—that, as every spiritually oriented person learns, are actually there for the perceiving, if only we quiet our hearts.

I have said I am not claiming reason can bring one to belief in God. What I am saying is this: Reason no longer stands in the way, as it once clearly did. The past two decades of research have overturned nearly all the important assumptions and predictions of an earlier generation of modern secular and atheist thinkers relating to the issue of God. Modern thinkers assumed that science would reveal the universe to be ever more random and mechanical; instead it has discovered unexpected new layers of intricate order that bespeak an almost unimaginably vast master design. Modern psychologists predicted that religion would be exposed as a neurosis and outgrown; instead, religious commitment has been shown empirically to be a vital component of basic mental health. Modern thinkers assumed that spirituality would be shown to have a physical basis; instead, something like the reverse has occurred: Health has been shown to have a spiritual underpinning. And, dogmatically, science and philosophy assumed that reason could never encounter evidence of a soul. But the application of modern research techniques to near-death studies has produced compelling data that no alternative hypothesis could explain.

"Some people learn from their mistakes," said Bismarck. "I on the other hand make it a practice to learn from the mistakes of others." Today, it seems to me, there is no good reason for an intelligent person to embrace the illusion of atheism or agnosticism, to make the same intellectual mistakes I made. I wish—how often do we say this in life?—that I had known then what I know now. That is my reason for writing this book—to lay out what seems to me the now overwhelming analytical case against the purely secular view of life, so that thinking skeptics can judge for themselves.

So having told my story, let me set forth my case. I believe you will find, as I have, that the road to the spiritual view of life—the process of filling what theologian Michael Novak has eloquently called "the empty shrine"[19] at the core of modern existence—is the greatest of intellectual, and human, adventures.

A
Not-So-Random
Universe

In the fall of 1973, the world's most eminent astronomers and physicists gathered in Poland to commemorate the 500th birthday of the father of modern astronomy, Nicolaus Copernicus. Assembled for the special two-week series of symposia were some of the most illustrious scientific minds of our time: Stephen W. Hawking, Roger Penrose, Robert Wagoner, Joseph Silk, and John Wheeler, to name only a few. The mood was festive. East-West détente was still in its heyday, and Poland's then-Communist government, bursting with pride at its favorite son Copernicus, rolled out the red carpet for its prestigious foreign guests. Participants were treated to a lavish reception and even a ballet. For the first half of September, scientists shuttled back and forth among Warsaw, Kraków, and Copernicus's birthplace of

Torun, taking in the sights, listening to countless lectures, comparing notes on the latest astronomical discoveries, and airing their newest cosmological speculations.[1]

Yet of the dozens of scientific lectures presented during the festivities, only one would be remembered decades later, echoing far beyond the hall in Kraków where it was delivered, indeed far beyond the field of astronomy or even science itself. Its author, Brandon Carter, was a well-established astrophysicist and cosmologist from Cambridge University, a close friend and sometime fellow graduate student of the (later) more famous Hawking. The title of the paper was technical-sounding and the tone of the presentation highly tentative. "Large Number Coincidences and the Anthropic Principle in Cosmology," Carter called it.[2] Yet there was nothing merely technical about the paper's implications. For the insights he presented, 500 years after Copernicus's birth, spelled nothing less than the philosophical overthrow of the Copernican revolution itself.

Carter called his notion the "anthropic principle," from the Greek word *anthropos,* "man." The name was a bit off-putting. And Carter's definition of the idea was highly technical. The anthropic principle consisted of the observation that "what we can expect to observe [in the universe] must be restricted by the conditions necessary for our presence as observers."[3] In plainer English, the anthropic principle says that all the seemingly arbitrary and unrelated constants in physics have one strange thing in common—these are precisely the values you need if you want to have a universe capable of producing life.

In essence, the anthropic principle came down to the observation that all the myriad laws of physics were fine-tuned from the very beginning of the universe for the creation of man—that the universe we inhabit appeared to be expressly designed for the emergence of human beings.

This discovery, already percolating among physicists in the early 1970s, came as something of a surprise, to put it mildly. For centuries, scientific exploration seemed to be taking us down precisely the opposite road—toward an ever more mechanistic, impersonal, and random view of the cosmos. Twentieth-century intellectuals had commonly spoken of the "random universe." The predominant view of modern philosophers and intellectuals was that human life had come about essentially by accident, the by-product of brute, material forces randomly churning over the eons. This conclusion seemed to follow naturally from the two great scientific revolutions of the modern era, the Copernican and the Darwinian. With his sun-centered model of the planetary system, Copernicus showed that humanity was not in any sense "central" to the universe. "Before the Copernican revolution, it was natural to suppose that God's purposes were specially concerned with the earth, but now this has become an unplausible hypothesis," the atheistic scientist Bertrand Russell wrote in his 1935 classic, *Religion and Science*.[4] Darwin, moreover, had demonstrated that the origins of life and even of the human species could be explained by blind mechanisms. In the wake of Copernicus and Darwin, it no longer seemed plausible to regard the universe as created or humanity as a creature of God. "Man" should rather be understood, as Russell expressed it, as some kind of unfortunate accident or sideshow in the material universe—"a curious accident in a backwater."[5]

The philosophical, cultural, and emotional impact of this conclusion could hardly be overstated. It explained the tone of despair and angst that came to characterize modern culture, the desperate feeling that humankind was alone and without moorings, and above all without God. It was this random universe cosmology that underpinned all the atheistic modern philosophies—from Russell's own positivism, to existentialism, Marxism, even Freudianism.

But then the unexpected occurred. Beginning in the 1960s, scientists began to notice a strange connection among a number of otherwise unexplained coincidences in physics. It turns out that many mysterious values and relationships in physics could be explained by one overriding fact: Such values had been necessary for the creation of life. The physicist Robert Dicke was the first to draw attention to this relationship.[6] The scientist John Wheeler, one of the most prestigious practitioners of cosmology, became interested in the idea in the 1960s.[7] Then, at Wheeler's urging, Carter presented the observation in full-blown form at the Copernican festivities.[8]

A SCIENTIFIC
EMBARRASSMENT

The anthropic principle offered a kind of explanation for one of the most basic mysteries of physics—the values of the fundamental constants.

Physicists had never been able to explain why the values of the so-called fundamental constants—for example, the values for the gravitational force or the electromagnetic force— were as they were. They were just "constants." One had to accept them. Moreover, there were certain mysterious mathematical relations among some of these constants. For example, the forces binding certain particles seemed to be mathematically related to the number for the age of the universe. Why should these forces be related to the age of the universe? In the past, physicists like Arthur Eddington and Paul Dirac had come up with some rather exotic theories to explain these coincidences.[9]

But there was a simpler way of explaining them, as Carter pointed out in his lecture. If one examined closely the evolution of the universe, one would see that these precise values or ratios were necessary if the universe was to be capable of producing life. In a certain sense, this finding was no surprise: We would not expect to be observing a universe that had not produced us in the first place. Still, the number of strange "coincidences" that could be explained simply because they were necessary for producing life in the universe was surprisingly large.

That was where Copernicus came in. People had interpreted Copernicus's theory to mean that humankind had no "privileged *central*" place in the universe, as Carter put it. But the explanation was not so simple. Too many values had seemingly been arranged around the central task of producing *us*. So, as Carter stated (in a somewhat hair-splitting fashion), even if our position in the universe was not "*central*," it was "inevitably privileged to some extent."[10]

Few people at the time seemed to be thinking deeply about the philosophical implications of this discovery.[11] But they were nothing short of astounding. In effect, the "random universe" was out the window. There was nothing random at all about the arrangement of the cosmos—as physicists quickly began to see. The vast, fifteen-billion-year evolution of the universe had apparently been directed toward one goal: the creation of human life.

The anthropic principle raised fundamental questions not only about the modern interpretation of Copernicanism, but ultimately about Darwinism as well. It certainly showed that Darwin's theory of "natural selection" could no longer be taken as an exhaustive explanation for the phenomenon of life. The notion that the whole process could be reduced to the workings of a single, simple "blind" mechanism was fundamentally flawed. The picture was vastly more complex than that.

The point is this: The "death of God" had been based on a fundamental *misinterpretation* of the nature of the universe, on a very partial and flawed picture that science had come up with by the late nineteenth century. Now that picture was being replaced by a new one, vastly more complex—and decisively more compatible with the notion that the universe had been designed by an intelligent Creator.

Indeed, what twentieth-century cosmology had come up with was something of a scientific embarrassment: a universe with a definite beginning, expressly designed for life. Ironically, the picture of the universe bequeathed to us by the most advanced twentieth-century science is closer in spirit to the vision presented in the Book of Genesis than anything offered by science since Copernicus. The irony is deepened by the fact that modern cosmology is the result of extending the concept of "evolution"—an idea once viewed as deeply inimical to faith.

THE PRIMEVAL ATOM

What made the discovery of the anthropic principle possible was the advent of big bang cosmology. At the time Russell wrote *Religion and Science,* nobody knew in a scientific sense how the universe had begun, or whether indeed it had a beginning. In the late 1920s the physicist Georges Lemaître proposed that the universe had originated in a primeval atom, but this was a highly controversial idea. Then in 1945 came the explosion of the atomic bomb. Shortly thereafter the physicist George Gamow (who had worked on the bomb project) proposed that the universe had originated in a similar original cataclysm.[12] The existence of the bomb—and the theories that went into understanding nuclear fission and especially nuclear fusion—gave this notion of an initial explosion greater credibility. The Lemaître-Gamow model accounted for one important mystery, the "red shift." In 1927, the astronomer Edwin Hubble had discovered that other galaxies are rapidly rushing away from ours (causing light from these galaxies to shift toward the red end of the color spectrum), that the universe is constantly expanding. The primeval atom theory—which envisioned the universe exploding out from an initial point—explained why that would be. But for roughly twenty years, scientists were divided between Gamow's theory and the so-called steady state universe, or the argument that the universe had always been there. It was Fred Hoyle, a leading proponent of the steady state theory, who coined the derisive term "big bang theory" to describe the position of his opponents.[13] The label stuck.

Then in 1964, a couple of scientists at Bell Laboratories, Arno Penzias and Robert W. Wilson, stumbled on what was later known as the cosmic background radiation. Penzias and Wilson, who were working on communication satellites, were annoyed to find low-level "noise" emanating from every direction in the sky. Physicists quickly realized what this noise was—an echo of the big bang billions of years before. It became apparent that the big bang theory was almost certainly right.[14]

Even before the big bang looked like a sure thing, scientists had been making considerable progress reconstructing the evolution of the universe from its (then) hypothetical beginnings. By the 1970s, with the big bang firmly established, physicists began to think about alternative scenarios for the universe's evolution. Say you tinkered with the value of gravity or altered very slightly the strength of the electromagnetic force—how would this affect the path of the universe's evolution? What they quickly found was that even the slightest tinkering with the values of physics derailed the whole process. Sometimes you ended up with the wrong kind of stars. In other cases you ended up with no stars at all. No matter what alternative scenario you tried to cook up, the most minuscule changes in the fundamental constants completely eliminated the possibility of life.[15]

Carter presented some of these points in his 1973 lecture. Any tinkering with the gravitational constant in relation to electromagnetism, he pointed out, would have resulted in a universe with no middling stars like our sun, but only cooler "red" or hotter "blue" ones—incapable of sustaining life's evolution. Any weakening of the nuclear "strong" force would have resulted in a universe consisting of hydrogen and not a single other element. That would mean no oxygen, no water, nothing but hydrogen.[16]

But these initial observations proved to be merely the tip of the iceberg. In the years following his lecture, Carter and other scientists would discover an increasingly daunting and improbable list of mysterious coincidences or "lucky accidents" in the universe—whose only common denominator seemed to be that they were necessary for our emergence. Even the most minor tinkering with the value of the fundamental forces of physics—gravity, electromagnetism, the nuclear strong force, or the nuclear weak force—would have resulted in an unrecognizable universe: a universe consisting entirely of helium, a universe without protons or atoms, a universe without stars, or a universe that collapsed back in upon itself before the first moments of its existence were up. Changing the precise ratios of the masses of subatomic particles in relation to one another would have similar effects. Even such basics of life as carbon and water depend upon uncanny "fine-tuning" at the subatomic level, strange coincidences in values for which physicists had no other explanation.

To take just a few examples:

- Gravity is roughly 10^{39} times weaker than electromagnetism. If gravity had been 10^{33} times weaker than electromagnetism, "stars would be a billion times less massive and would burn a million times faster."[17]
- The nuclear weak force is 10^{28} times the strength of gravity. Had the weak force been slightly weaker, all the hydrogen in the universe would have been turned to helium (making water impossible, for example).[18]
- A stronger nuclear strong force (by as little as 2 percent) would have prevented the formation of protons—yielding a universe without atoms. Decreasing it by 5 percent would have given us a universe without stars.[19]
- If the difference in mass between a proton and a neutron were not exactly as it is—roughly twice the mass of

an electron—then all neutrons would have become protons or vice versa. Say good-bye to chemistry as we know it—and to life.[20]

- The very nature of water—so vital to life—is something of a mystery (a point noticed by one of the forerunners of anthropic reasoning in the nineteenth century, Harvard biologist Lawrence Henderson). Unique among the molecules, water is lighter in its solid than liquid form: Ice floats. If it did not, the oceans would freeze from the bottom up and earth would now be covered with solid ice. This property in turn is traceable to unique properties of the hydrogen atom.[21]

- The synthesis of carbon—the vital core of all organic molecules—on a significant scale involves what scientists view as an "astonishing" coincidence in the ratio of the strong force to electromagnetism.[22] This ratio makes it possible for carbon-12 to reach an excited state of exactly 7.65 MeV at the temperature typical of the center of stars, which creates a resonance involving helium-4, beryllium-8, and carbon-12—allowing the necessary binding to take place during a tiny window of opportunity 10^{-17} seconds long.

The list goes on. A comprehensive compilation of these coincidences can be found in John Leslie's book *Universes*.[23]

The depth of the mystery involved here has been captured best by astronomer Fred Hoyle, the former proponent of the steady state theory:

All that we see in the universe of observation and fact, as opposed to the mental state of scenario and supposition, remains unexplained. And even in its supposedly first second the universe itself is acausal. That is to say, the universe has to know in advance what it is going to be before it knows how to start itself. For in accordance with the Big Bang Theory, for instance, at a time of 10^{-43} seconds the universe has to know how many types of neutrino there are going to be at a time of 1 second. This is so in order that it starts off expanding at the right rate to fit the eventual number of neutrino types.[24]

Hoyle's notion of the universe needing to "know in advance" later outcomes captures the depth of the mystery. The fine-tuning of seemingly heterogeneous values and ratios necessary to get from the big bang to life as we know it involves intricate coordination over vast differences in scale—from the galactic level down to the subatomic one—and across multibillion-year tracts of time. Hoyle, who coined the term "big bang," has questioned the very legitimacy of the metaphor of an initial "explosion." "An explosion in a junkyard does not lead to sundry bits of metal being assembled into a useful working machine," he writes.[25] The more physicists have learned about the universe, the more it looks like a put-up job.

THE RISE AND FALL OF MECHANISM

This has not been a particularly happy realization for the scientific community. Yes, in a sense you could say that the anthropic principle "explained" all these mysterious coincidences, but it was a very unscientific sort of explanation. It was, in essence, a "teleological" explanation—the kind of explanation that the old natural philosophers used to offer for things, before modern science came along.[26] The word *teleology* comes from the Greek word *telos* meaning "end" or "goal." Aristotle thought it was a sufficient explanation of something to say that its end or goal *caused* it. He called this the "final cause." For example, an oak tree (or rather its "essence" or "nature") is the final cause of the path of growth that begins with the acorn. The essence of the flower is the final cause of the process that begins with the seed. The essence or nature of the adult human being is the final cause of the process that begins with the fetus in the womb.[27]

This form of thinking is now quite alien to us, since our view of the world is conditioned by modern science. We don't even use the word *cause* in this sense anymore. Modern science is not interested in the final cause. It looks rather for the efficient cause, the mechanism that actually brings things about. The anthropic principle harks back to the older style of thinking. In effect, the anthropic principle says that humanity is (apparently) the final cause of the universe. The most basic explanation of the universe is that it seems to be a process orchestrated to achieve the end or goal of creating human beings. This explanation is not a scientific explanation in the modern sense of that term.

Modern science was born when human beings abandoned talk of final causes and began to look exclusively for "efficient causes," for the underlying mechanisms that explained "how" things "worked." The great transition to modern science occurred in the battle over Copernicus's theory—the Copernican revolution. Galileo was the hero of this great battle. He claimed that the observations of the heavens he had made with his new telescope vindicated Copernicus's theory: Contrary to what people had thought for centuries, the sun was fixed and the earth orbited around it and rotated on an axis. This novel idea was extremely annoying to the natural philosophers of Galileo's day, who were basically followers of Aristotle. Some of them actually conspired against Galileo to get the Church to silence him and ultimately convict him as a heretic.[28] In so doing, of course, the Church forever discredited its doctrines in the minds of many thinking people. It sacrificed its claim that it had a monopoly on the truth.

Galileo was punished (with a sentence of life imprisonment, quickly commuted to lifelong house arrest) and his books officially banned (he later found a publisher in Protestant Holland). But his ideas triumphed, and with them came the end of Aristotelian science and the search for final causes. Modern science was the triumph of *mechanism* over *teleology* and remained so until this century. In time, scientists were able to elaborate more and more mechanisms to explain how the universe and everything we see around us worked. All the mysteries that human beings had once attributed to God or the gods turned out to have simple mechanistic explanations.

The rise of mechanism went hand in hand with the decline of religious faith among the intellectual elite. One could see this happening even in the writings of the earliest great theorists of science—for example, Descartes, who more or less reduced God to a mathematical abstraction, and even Newton, who, though publicly very pious, was privately tortured and doubtful.[29] As the mechanistic explanation expanded, it left increasingly little room for God. By the eighteenth century, theism—or the belief in a personal God—had given way to deism—or the view of God as simply the "first cause" and underlying principle of rationality in the universe.[30] The most famous eighteenth-century deist, Voltaire, openly attacked religion. Deism quickly deteriorated into atheism, or the belief in no God at all. Such was the position of the English philosopher David Hume and of the later generation of French *philosophes,* such as Baron d'Holbach and Denis Diderot.[31] The French thinkers were particularly open and aggressive in their attacks on religious belief—partly because of the still powerful role that the Catholic Church played in French politics.

Nonetheless, until the nineteenth century, the vast majority of people and even a significant portion of the intellectual elite remained religious believers. Then came the final blow: the coming of age of the two "historical" sciences, geology and biology. In the early nineteenth century, many scientists still thought the Old Testament gave a literal account of the early history of the world, and they came up with a history of the earth based on the first books of the Bible. They computed the age of the earth from the biblical genealogies (modern "Creationists" or "young-earth" theorists try to do this today; however, unlike their predecessors, they do not have the excuse of scientific ignorance to justify such absurdities). They explained the irregularities of the earth with reference to Noah's flood. The theory was known as *catastrophism*—based on the catastrophe of the Biblical deluge—and its proponents saw it explicitly as a way of vindicating belief in God with reference to nature. In 1830, Charles Lyell's book *Principles of Geology* blew the catastrophists out of the water. In three volumes of meticulous argumentation, Lyell showed how the normal forces of nature could account for all the irregularities of the natural landscape—so long as one assumed that the earth was vastly older than the Bible stories suggested. It indeed was older, according to Lyell. The fossil record showed that whole species of creatures had arisen, lived, and fallen extinct. No catastrophic floods or other such divine intervention had been necessary to produce the irregularities we see in the natural landscape. There was a purely mechanistic explanation for the history of the earth.[32]

Lyell's geology did to the Protestant world what Galileo's discoveries had done to the Catholic one. It was a terrible blow to religious belief. (Interestingly, in both cases, the culprit on religion's side was an unwise insistence on biblical literalism in the face of scientific proof to the contrary—a strategy that St. Augustine had warned against as early as A.D. 415.)[33] By the middle of the nineteenth century, even before Darwin's blockbuster book, educated people were finding it extremely difficult to reconcile the discoveries of the new science with religious faith.[34] The trauma could be seen in the work of Victorian England's most popular poet, Alfred Tennyson, who described a new vision of nature as "red in tooth and claw." The famous phrase came from *In Memoriam,* a series of plaintive lyrics in which the poet tries to come to terms with the untimely death of his closest friend, in light of what modern science had shown about the mechanical coldness and indifference of the universe. Whole species or "types" had perished from the earth:

> *Are God and Nature then at strife,*
> *That Nature lends such evil dreams?*
> *So careful of the type she seems,*
> *So careless of the single life. . . .*
>
> *"So careful of the type?" but no.*
> *From scarped cliff and quarried stone*
> *She cries, "A thousand types are gone:*
> *I care for nothing, all shall go." . . .*

And he, shall he,
Man, her last work, who seemed so fair . . .

Who trusted God was love indeed
And love Creation's final law
Tho' Nature, red in tooth and claw,
With ravine, shriek'd against his creed

. . . Be blown about the desert dust,
Or sealed within the iron hills?

Or again, there was the novelist George Eliot's famous remark to a friend about the three great "inspiring trumpet-calls of men . . . *God, Immortality, Duty,*" of which she said, "how inconceivable was the *first,* how unbelievable was the *second,* and yet how peremptory and absolute the *third.*"[35] The German atheistic philosopher Ludwig Feuerbach was more blunt. People did yet not realize it, he wrote in 1850, but natural science had "long before dissolved the Christian world view in nitric acid."[36]

Victorians of Eliot's and Tennyson's generation experienced what the scholar J. Hillis Miller once called "the disappearance of God."[37] But it was Darwin who appeared to seal the "death."

The young Darwin took the first volume of Lyell's *Principles of Geology* along on his famous voyage on the *Beagle* in 1831. He went into the voyage a Bible-believing Christian; within a short time after the voyage, he was agnostic.[38] He would not publish *The Origin of Species* until 1859. When it appeared, it was the *coup de grâce:* Modern science had at last found a simple mechanism to explain the origin of life and the human species itself.

T. H. Huxley, the leading apostle of Darwinism, later described the dramatic impact of Darwin's book:

> The *Origin* . . . did the immense service of freeing us forever from the dilemma—Refuse to accept the Creation hypothesis, and what have you to propose that can be accepted by any cautious reasoner? In 1857 I had no answer ready, and I do not think that anyone else had. A year later we reproached ourselves with dulness [*sic*] for being perplexed with such an enquiry. My reflection when I first made myself master of the central idea of the Origin, was, "How extremely stupid not to have thought of that!"[39]

Darwin breathed fresh life into the atheist position—a fact immediately recognized across the globe. Notably, that other famous nineteenth-century atheist, Karl Marx, asked Darwin if he could dedicate the English translation of *Capital* to the great naturalist, a request that Darwin, partly in deference to the sensitivities of his pious Christian wife, refused.[40] Huxley coined the term *agnostic* to describe his position vis-à-vis the question of God, a term that Darwin later adopted to describe his own.[41]

Science, it appeared, had found mechanistic explanations for *everything*. The verdict seemed inescapable. It was uttered finally in 1885 by the German philosopher Friedrich Nietzsche, the philosophical "shock jock" of his era: "God is dead."[42]

Moderns of the era of Friedrich Nietzsche, and later Bertrand Russell and Sigmund Freud, were convinced that this mechanistic vision of the cosmos was the last word. Neither Russell nor Freud nor Marx nor Nietzsche would ever have expected that the mechanistic model itself might be overturned.

The "modern" era in science and philosophy could essentially be defined as the era of the triumph of mechanism over teleology. The defining feature of modern thinking was that in it mechanism always had the upper hand. For this reason, the advent of the anthropic principle is a much more momentous event in Western intellectual history than many people have realized. Suddenly, for the first time since Galileo, teleology has trumped mechanism—and on the biggest and most fundamental question imaginable, the nature of the universe itself. For the first time in over 350 years, science is at a loss to reduce the universe and the order we see around us to mechanistic principles. Indeed, it is growing increasingly doubtful whether the anthropic principle can be explained away in mechanistic terms *even in principle,* as we shall see. Some scientists (focusing on parallel mysteries that have simultaneously opened up in the field of quantum mechanics) have spoken of the "death of materialism."[43] The change we are witnessing is even more profound than that. The great modern era—spanning the nearly 350 years between the trial of Galileo and the 500th birthday of Copernicus—is at an end. It is truly justifiable to speak of our current period as the "postmodern age." And there is every reason to suppose that this postmodern age will also be postsecular, since the original philosophical assumptions underpinning the modern secular worldview have been shattered—ironically enough, by science itself.

THE POPE AND THE PHYSICISTS

Modern science, of course, has hardly given up the ghost. The search continues for an alternative explanation for the universe's mysteries. Indeed, many scientists are inclined to regard the anthropic principle less as an explanation than as the absence of an explanation, a pitiful confession of scientific ignorance.[44] The search for an alternative answer moves on two separate but interrelated tracks. First, there is the effort to find a theory to unify the fundamental forces, a so-called theory of everything. If physics arrived at a theory of everything, the fundamental constants would disappear. There would no longer be a need for unexplained constants, since physics would understand the underlying principle or mechanism that determines why the various forces and subatomic realities of nature take the values that they do. Instead of unexplained, fixed constants, physicists would have *equations* explaining the interrelations among the fundamental forces. If there were no longer any constants, there could be no coincidences among constants. There would be no coincidences whatsoever. In a theory of everything, everything would be explained.

At present there is a theory that seems to unify three out of the four fundamental forces—electromagnetism, the strong force, and the weak force. Gravity, however, remains unaccounted for, the elephant still outside the tent.

The alternative strategy is to come up with a more complete cosmology, a more satisfying *mechanism* to account for why the universe takes the remarkable form that it does.[45] The most-talked-about innovation in cosmology today is known as the inflation theory, which raised everybody's hopes a few years ago by seeming to explain two of the important anthropic coincidences: the so-called flatness and smoothness problems. But inflation, a still highly speculative theory, has rapidly encountered new problems of its own.[46]

As recently as a decade ago, there was a good deal of optimism among physicists that a unified theory might be in sight.[47] Today a certain mood of pessimism seems to be setting in. As the physicist Steven Weinberg recently observed, somewhat disconsolately, in *The New York Review of Books,* "As we make progress understanding the expanding universe, the problem itself expands, so that the solution always seems to recede from us."[48]

Today, moreover, the physicists find themselves constantly looking over their shoulder at the theologians, who watch with intrigue as the scientists are forced to wrestle anew with an issue they thought they had put to rest a long time ago: God. (Thus we find the physicist Weinberg feeling compelled to quote the Jewish philosopher Maimonides and mention St. Augustine in his recent review of scientific cosmology books for *The New York Review,* insisting, essentially, that the theologians are *still* wrong!)

One can discern two somewhat different motives in the strivings of the physicists and cosmologists today. One is a purely professional impulse. A scientist is one who is paid to offer mechanistic explanations for the universe, and the best scientists are more than happy simply to do what they are paid to do. But side by side with the professional impulse, a certain ideological mission has crept in. Many scientists are profoundly uncomfortable with the universe of the new cosmology, precisely because it leaves such ample room for God. The whole picture is damnably disconcerting: a universe with a beginning, designed for man. Many scientists want this picture to go away.

The famous cosmologist Stephen W. Hawking decided to try to solve the first part of the problem by getting rid of the beginning of the universe. He did so in preparation for a major international conference on scientific cosmology in

1981, sponsored by—of all places—the Vatican. The willingness of the Church of Rome to play host to an assembly of contemporary physicists doubtless had something to do with the Vatican's sense that the scientific winds were suddenly and delightfully shifting in its favor. Pope John Paul II, no *naïf* when it comes to the ins and outs of modern science and philosophy, seized tellingly on the weakness of the scientists' case in his address to the conference:

> Any scientific hypothesis on the origin of the world, such as that of a primeval atom from which the whole of the physical world derived, leaves open the problem concerning the beginning of the Universe. Science cannot by itself resolve such a question: what is needed is that human knowledge that rises above physics and astrophysics and which is called metaphysics; it needs above all the knowledge that comes from the revelation of God.[49]

One could sense a kind of quiet revenge here for the embarrassment caused to the Church hundreds of years earlier by the Galileo affair. For the scientists' part, that they would find themselves in the position of being lectured (literally and figuratively) by the pope cannot have seemed a comfortable, or entirely fair, position at which to arrive after so much spectacular scientific progress toward penetrating the deepest mysteries of the universe. One would not expect them to take it sitting down. In a sense, they didn't.

At this very conference, Hawking introduced his famous "no-boundary" proposal, designed to eliminate the universe's beginning. Essentially, the Hawking proposal—later refined in collaboration with Jim Hartle—eliminated the temporal beginning point by placing the universe in a larger superspace comprising real plus (mathematically) "imaginary time." In a sense it was a way of "getting outside" the universe so that $t = 0$, or the beginning, was not a point on a linear time line but rather, by analogy, a point on a sphere, like the north pole on a globe. In this sense, there would be nothing "before" $t = 0$ and, moreover, the point $t = 0$ would be "nothing special." Lest anyone doubt that Hawking's motivation may have had less to do with the demands of science than with the challenge of theology, Hawking himself has been clear on the point. "So long as the universe had a beginning," he wrote in *A Brief History of Time*, "we could suppose it had a creator. But if the universe is really completely self-contained, having no boundary or edge, it would have neither beginning nor end: It would simply be. What place, then, for a creator?"[50]

These physicists, one is forced to admit, are clever fellows, and there is no question but that Hawking's framework provided an ingenious answer to the simple argument raised by the pope. But Hawking's theory has remained controversial. And, more important, it did not solve the larger problem, which lay in the anthropic coincidences. As the Oxford theologian Keith Ward has pointed out, "What the Hartle-Hawking theory leaves unexplained is why the basic quantum fields, the boundary conditions of the cosmos, should be as they are, why the physical laws should be as they are, and how it is that the laws give the appearance of existing objectively and 'governing' the sorts of events that come into being."[51]

From the scientists' viewpoint, the fact that the universe looks as though it had a definite beginning might be upsetting enough. But what appears to drive cosmologists nearly to distraction is the anthropic principle. Again and again, scientific authorities seek to banish it from the halls of science. Again and again, it pops up at scientific meetings in the mouth of some prominent cosmologist.[52] It is a "can't live with it, can't live without it" situation. On the one hand, the principle smacks of a pre-Copernican anthropocentrism—precisely the intellectual ailment of which modern science had supposedly cured us—and, worse, of theism—of which modern science was *really* supposed to have cured us. On the other hand, it can be used effectively to make scientifically verifiable predictions.[53] Certainly, the effort to explain, or explain away, the anthropic coincidences has been a major factor keeping cosmologists in business these past twenty years. Some of the most imaginative speculation in modern cosmology is motivated by a desire to remove this particular zebra from the front parlor of science.

MONKEY BUSINESS

How does one do that? It is not clear that even a theory of everything would solve the problem. Even if one could find an underlying mechanism to unify the constants, the larger philosophical issue might remain: How does one explain that the laws of physics fit so perfectly with the fifteen-billion-year project of creating life?

So a theory of everything offers little consolation to scientists; and in any case, it appears to be a long way off. Instead, the battle has been fought largely on the terrain of cosmology itself. The main strategy of the physicists for discounting the anthropic principle is to *multiply imaginary universes*. The reasoning behind this strategy is fairly simple: If there were an infinite number (or, in the late Carl Sagan's favorite phrase, "billions and billions") of other universes, then the fact that ours hit on the right combination of physical laws to produce the miracle of life might not be such a miracle after all—or so the argument goes. Humanity would again become an "accident."

We should begin by noting that none of these imaginary universes about which cosmologists ceaselessly speculate these days have been shown to exist. They are pure products of scientific imagination. Moreover, because they are alternative universes, they would seem to be inherently undetectable. That raises difficulties enough. But there is a further problem—the question of whether random variation could even *in principle* create the vast order that pervades the one universe we know.

In its generic form, the idea that randomness, over time, will eventually produce order has a very old pedigree, long predating modern science. It was used by the Epicureans of Roman times to justify their atheism and was later revived by the eighteenth-century atheist philosophers Denis Diderot and David Hume: Given infinite time, nature would by chance alone eventually hit on the order we see around us.[54] The modern version of the argument often takes the form of an analogy (as far as one can tell, first introduced into modern scientific discourse by the famous Eddington):[55] Given infinite time, a monkey with a typewriter would eventually type the works of Shakespeare.

But would he? Would he not more likely produce an infinity's worth of gibberish? It is worth pausing to examine the logic here, for the famous "monkey thesis" contains a large, and highly questionable, metaphysical presupposition. Imagine that your job for the rest of infinite time was to act as supervisor for this particular monkey. And let us suppose that the powers that be were decent enough to give you and the monkey an eight-hour day—an infinity of eight-hour days. Each morning you would get up and go to the office, where the monkey would faithfully sit down at the typewriter and type. Each day, at the end, you would read over what the monkey had produced. Doubtless you would find the occasional English word, maybe even a short sentence or two; now and again there might even be something approaching two sentences in rough logical sequence, though anything approaching a grammatical sequence of sentences would be extremely rare. Even where you found recognizable English, you would find errors. Then suppose one evening you began to read and found:

EGEON

Proceed, Solinus, to procure my fall,
And by the doom of death end woes and all.

DUKE

Merchant of Syracusa, plead no more.
I am not partial to infringe our laws. . . .

And let us say that the text went on in this fashion sequentially in accord with the text of the play usually placed first in Shakespeare's collected works—appropriately, perhaps, *The Comedy of Errors*. What would be your assumption? That this was purely coincidence, the entirely expected outcome of random monkey-typing over time? That you had had one too many monkey-typing days and were finally losing your marbles? Let us say that you could establish that you were sane and that the monkey, unassisted, had indeed typed this very text. What would you think? You would think it was a miracle.

The point is that it does not matter if there is an infinity of days. Each morning, the situation, and the problem, is the same. Where is the agency that would provide the order required for even a day's worth of typing of Shakespeare, let alone the complete works? The monkey thesis is, in effect, a *Groundhog Day* situation—to recall the well-known Bill Murray movie where the same day, and the same set of problems, repeats itself again and again. It is a gross fallacy to suppose that the quantity of days or time available changes anything. (To put the proposition mathematically, the probability on any given day that the monkey will type the works of Shakespeare—or anything equivalently meaningful, extensive, and ordered—is not one in some very, very large number; it is zero.) Randomness does not engender order on any appreciable scale, no matter how many billions of years or opportunities you give it. And the works of Shakespeare, though complex enough, are small potatoes next to the universe.

The view that randomness engenders order is not a conclusion but an *assumption* of the modern scientific and philosophic worldview—dating from the days when mechanism seemed to have completely explained away teleology. It is a groundless and question-begging assumption. It expresses little more than an a priori metaphysical preference for a godless cosmos.

This assumption about randomness creating order seemed to find support in nature solely through Darwin's theory of natural selection. Darwin's theory seemed to overcome what philosophers had until then seen as a great barrier to a purely mechanistic explanation of nature. In his famous "third critique," the *Critique of Judgment,* the eighteenth-century

German philosopher Immanuel Kant had argued that mechanism can explain everything in the world but two: beauty and organisms.[56] You might call this "the flower problem." Kant's argument could be boiled down to the question, "Why are there flowers?" Or, to put it differently, "If God does not exist, then how do you explain the existence of flowers?" Darwin's theory *seemed* to solve this problem once and for all.

But the problem is that Darwin's theory, too, is now fraying at the seams. Not that mainstream biologists are prepared to abandon natural selection or even to rob it of all of its supposed "creative" capabilities to create order. (We will see where this stands in ten years; Thomas Kuhn explained why threatened "paradigms" in science are slow to fall;[57] evolutionary biology gives every indication of being in the early stages of a "paradigm shift," as natural selection is increasingly qualified and overshadowed by other ideas.) But even among the most mainstream biologists a consensus is growing that natural selection cannot by itself explain the order of the biological world. There is also a clear recognition that the patterns in the fossil record do not accord with the patterns Darwin would have predicted. No less an authority than Harvard paleontologist Stephen Jay Gould has attacked what he calls the "Darwinian fundamentalists," writers like Daniel Dennett and Richard Dawkins, for insisting that the mechanism of natural selection holds the entire key to evolution. Recent discoveries have been in the opposite direction—toward recognizing what Gould calls "an astonishing 'conservation'" in basic evolutionary "pathways." In other words, biologists are emphasizing that the manner in which organisms evolve is determined more by internal dicta than by simple adaptation to the outside world. Definite "pathways" are built into the organic world, and organisms evolve according to these pathways. Order is not created simply by random trial and adaptation. It comes from somewhere else. Moreover, in contrast to what Darwin would have predicted, the fossil record does not show gradual, steady change over time, but rather long periods of "stability" punctuated by sharp jolts of change—a pattern Gould has called "punctuated equilibrium." Natural selection cannot account for this.[58] In short, natural selection is not the magic bullet biologists once thought it was: You can't explain away the order in nature by reference to a purely random process. This is to say nothing of the anthropic coincidences, which are necessary for life and about which biology has nothing to say. (Notably, the "Darwinian fundamentalists" are also the writers who have argued most vociferously that Darwin's "dangerous idea" of natural selection was the final refutation of God.)[59]

So the revolution that we first witnessed in cosmology is now beginning to shake biology. Late-twentieth-century science has overturned the assumptions that reigned at the end of the nineteenth century. In one sense, this revolution should come as no surprise. Had it not been for the peculiar prestige of science, and Darwin's overstatement of his case, human beings might have recognized on the basis of their ordinary experience of the natural world what seems an obvious truth: Randomness alone cannot produce order on any appreciable scale.

SCIENCE FICTION

But back to the imaginary universes of the physicists. A final problem with these imaginary universes is that the physicists keep finding them in different places. First we had "parallel universes." Then came "baby universes." Now there is talk of "bubble universes." The current universe is so wonderfully ordered and mysterious that many physicists suddenly seem to feel a need to find other, less ordered, ones to explain the current one away.

They first looked for these other universes in the bizarre, fun-house world of quantum mechanics. Quantum mechanics poses an entire set of fresh mysteries, which are beyond the scope of this book. Suffice it to say that in quantum mechanics it often seems as if things can *be* and *not be* at the same time. When you penetrate to the deepest level of matter, it stops behaving like matter as we know it. There's nothing solid or definite about it. The most famous illustration of the quantum paradoxes was Erwin Schrödinger's well-known analogy of the cat. The cat is stuck in a box with a vial of poison gas to be triggered in turn by radioactive decay. (Schrödinger was doubtless a "dog person.") The poison vial may be shattered, or it may not be, depending on quantum probabilities. According to the mainstream interpretation of quantum mechanics, the cat is mysteriously suspended between the life and death states—neither dead nor alive—until the scientist opens the box and *observes* him, at which point he *becomes* alive or dead, as a result of the *observation*. None of this makes any sense, which was part of Schrödinger's point. In 1957 a young doctoral student, Hugh Everett, proposed an ingenious and fantastic solution to this paradox (the paradox is known in quantum mechanics as "the problem of measurement"). Everett proposed that all the possibilities implicit in matter before it is actually observed—before, for example, light in its fuzzy "wave" state is observed and collapses into a photon particle—actually exist in reality. Everett imagined that, at each observation, reality was infinitely branching out. My eye would observe one photon with certain properties in this universe, while, in effect, copies of "me" would be observing photons with the other possible properties in a series of parallel universes ad infinitum. So in some universes the cat would be dead and in others he would be alive. It just would depend what universe the scientist branched into upon observation.[60] This solution to the paradox was ingenious, but of course it amounted to a grand new paradox of its own.

Paul Davies and John Gribbin write that "many scientists" find the "parallel universes" idea "a preferable hypothesis to supernatural design."[61] But it is an odd sort of preference for scientists, given that these supposed extra universes are purely speculative, undetected, and undetectable in principle. The idea that the anthropic principle would be decisively explained away by appealing to the existence of infinite invisible universes that we shall never have an opportunity to observe, and whose existence can therefore never be established, is not exactly persuasive argumentation. Notably, the most prestigious proponent of the many universes (sometimes called "many worlds" or "many histories") idea—the famous American scientist John Wheeler, who was Everett's doctoral advisor—eventually abandoned the interpretation on grounds that "there's too much metaphysical baggage being carried along with it" and that it makes "science into a kind of mysticism."[62]

Mysticism, indeed. The final defense against the anthropic principle has come increasingly in the form of scientific myth making, the concocting of ever more spectacular speculative constructs that might in some way escape the more obvious implication of the cosmic coincidences—namely, that the cosmos is the product of an intelligent creator. These mythical constructs by and large lack empirical foundation and are not falsifiable by any current science; they rest on unproved hypothesis piled upon unproved hypothesis.

As the "many universes" idea has lost its luster, it has been succeeded by the "baby universes" proposal. Hawking has argued that when a black hole collapses into a singularity, a new baby universe can form whose four space-time dimensions exist at right angles to the existing one.[63] This proposal, though it has some mathematical foundation, is already controversial. No matter. Another physicist, Lee Smolin, has vastly embellished on Hawking's original speculation to provide what the prominent astrophysicist and science writer John Gribbin has characterized as the latest "counter-argument" to the anthropic principle.[64] I assume he is serious. But Smolin's wild series of suppositions makes Hugh Everett's bold "parallel universes" speculation look like dull common sense by comparison.

Smolin imagines Hawking's baby universes—expected to be an infinitesimal 10^{-25} centimeters in diameter—growing up. Smolin supposes that some of these baby universes *might* (presuming they existed in the first place, which has not been established) experience "inflation" of the sort that *some* cosmologists argue occurred in our own in the very first instants of the big bang. They would become massive universes like ours. He further theorizes that the very laws of physics *may* change slightly as particles pass through the imagined "wormhole" of the singularity into the new universe (another controversial proposition, to put it mildly). To this already highly speculative brew, he adds the spice of James Lovelock's controversial Gaia theory[65]—the claim, not very widely accepted as you might imagine, that the earth is in reality a single living organism. Smolin's aim is to arrive at a new theory of "natural selection" involving whole (mind you, as yet entirely imaginary) universes, thus bringing Darwin's principle of radical contingency smack dab back into the center of cosmology. The goal here is obvious: to resuscitate science's "old-time religion" of the random universe.

In a 1993 book titled *In the Beginning* (and thus presumably meant to offer contemporary cosmology's answer to the Book of Genesis), Gribbin offers a popularized version of Smolin's vision, originally set forth in an article in the journal *Classical and Quantum Gravity*.[66] In Gribbin's book, we are asked to accept the following propositions: not only that the earth is in fact a single living organism (Gaia), but also that each galaxy is literally a living organism; that the universe is a living organism; that our universe was once a "baby universe" in another universe; that our universe is seeding new "baby universes" in turn via black holes; and that the purpose of the whole exercise is not to create human beings, but to manufacture new universes (mind you, universes that have so far been shown to exist only in the minds of Smolin and Gribbin)—a process of which life in all its complexity was merely an accidental by-product. This is all very nice, of course, but not a shred of it rests on established fact. Smolin's great "counterargument" to the anthropic principle? He suggests that the universe may be optimized not to produce life, as dull anthropic reasoners had previously supposed, but rather to produce black holes.

So *there's* the answer to the anthropic mystery: The whole fifteen-billion-year exercise, intricately fine-tuned from the first 10^{-43} seconds to produce intelligent life eons later, was nothing more than an inexplicable accident on the path of the universe's *real* purpose, which is to maximize production of black holes. (Who put that purpose there? we may ask.) Of course, this proposition, and the lengthy list of "ifs" from which it hangs, is not only extremely "speculative," to use Smolin's own words from the journal article;[67] it is not even capable of even being tested by contemporary science. There is another speculative vision—also based on inflation theory—that similarly imagines "bubble universes" with alternative fundamental constants.[68]

Praising science at the expense of religion in 1935, Bertrand Russell boasted: "The scientific temper of mind is cautious, tentative, and piecemeal. The way in which science arrives at its beliefs is quite different," he wrote, "from that of medieval theology. . . . Science starts, not from large assumptions, but from particular facts discovered by observation or experiment."[69] Well, we've come a long way, baby.

THE POSTSECULAR UNIVERSE

Few people seem to realize this, but by now it should be clear: Over the course of a century in the great debate between science and faith, the tables have completely turned. In the wake of Darwin, atheists and agnostics like Huxley and Russell could point to what appeared to be a solid body of testable theory purportedly showing life to be accidental and the universe radically contingent. Many scientists and intellectuals continue to cleave to this worldview. But they are increasingly pressed to almost absurd lengths to defend it. Today the concrete data point strongly in the direction of the God hypothesis. It is the simplest and most obvious solution to the anthropic puzzle. (Can any scientist really believe that the

Gaia hypothesis is more reasonable?) Those who wish to oppose it have no testable theory to marshal, only speculations about unseen universes spun from the fertile scientific imagination. Smolin writes that the anthropic principle "has no explanatory power, given that we exclude explanation by final cause."[70] That is a fancy way of saying that the God hypothesis is by definition unscientific. It may be. But if it is, then modern science must surrender its long-standing pretension that it can supply answers to the ultimate questions. For one of the most important possible answers—and seemingly the most likely one based on the available evidence—has been ruled out from the start.

Not all scientists by any means take Hawking's, Gribbin's, or Smolin's side of the argument. Certainly, astronomer Fred Hoyle has given the anthropic principle its due. Paul Davies is an example of a physicist who, after dispassionately reviewing the evidence, has come down generally on the side of the hypothesis of design.[71] Moreover, there is a new school of scientist-theologians, fully credentialed in both fields—figures such as John Polkinghorne, Arthur Peacocke, and Robert John Russell—who have been doing their best to inform the public of the realities of the postsecular world: that the age-old scientific challenge to faith has simply collapsed.[72]

Modern science's discovery of the random universe was analogous to Columbus's "discovery" of the Indies—only later did it become clear that the world was a little bigger than the great explorer supposed and that he had stumbled not on Asia, but on a new continent. Science took somewhat longer—centuries, in fact—to expand its first glimpses of the natural order to a broader picture of the whole. As recently as twenty-five years ago, a reasonable person weighing the purely scientific evidence on the issue would likely have come down on the side of skepticism. That is no longer the case. The burden of proof has shifted. The barrier that modern science appeared to erect to faith has fallen. Of course, the anthropic principle tells us nothing about the Person of God or the existence of an after-life; it has nothing to say about such issues as right or wrong or the "problem of evil." But it does offer as strong an indication as reason and science alone could be expected to provide that God exists.

Psyche and Soul: Postsecularism in Psychology

fter Darwin and the random universe, the second great challenge to religious belief in the twentieth century came from Sigmund Freud and psychoanalysis. Psychoanalysis was a major force for secularization in twentieth-century societies, inspiring a virtual revolution in manners and morals. It was also an explicitly atheistic, indeed openly antireligious, doctrine. Freud attacked religious belief repeatedly. In *The Future of an Illusion* (1927), he branded faith as a form of mental disorder, a "universal obsessional neurosis," rooted in "infantile" and "narcissistic" patterns of thought—a neurosis that he predicted humanity would "outgrow."[1]

Not all psychoanalysts were as militantly atheistic as the master: Freud's disciple-turned-rival Carl Jung was a notable exception in viewing religion as a beneficial psychological force. But Freud's jaded view of religious belief shaped the majority outlook of the mental health profession, especially in the United States. In 1975, an American Psychiatric Association task force reported that a bare 43 percent of American psychiatrists believed in God—as compared to roughly 95 percent of the American population as a whole. The figures for the American Psychological Association were even more striking. A 1972 poll showed that a mere 1.1 percent of psychologists were believers.[2] Freud was not the only thinker responsible for this state of affairs. Some of the most important non-Freudian psychological theorists were also outspoken atheists. For example, B. F. Skinner, a founder of the behaviorist school, was a militant nonbeliever.[3] Albert Ellis, the founder of rational-emotive therapy, wrote extensively on religion as a cause of disease.[4] In a society rushing headlong toward secularization, psychoanalysis and psychology were among the most important bastions of unbelief.

Other psychological theorists may have criticized religion, but it was Freud who set the tone for the profession and gave it its atheistic stamp. The justification he presented for his antireligious position was, of course, science. As he wrote to his friend and frequent correspondent on religious issues, the Lutheran pastor and psychoanalyst Oskar Pfister, "[Psycho]analysis produces no new world view. But it does not need one, for it rests on the general scientific world view with which the religious one remains incompatible."[5] The notion of the incompatibility between religion and science—so integral to the modernist outlook after Darwin—became a central pillar of Freud's thought. As early as 1899 he spoke of the "new religion of science" supplanting the "old religion."[6] Freud went further, however, than many modern agnostics.

His thought absorbed something of the destructive flavor of the nineteenth century's most militantly antireligious thinkers, Ludwig Feuerbach and Friedrich Nietzsche.[7] Freud's approach to religion was aggressive; he was ever on the attack. If science was to prosper, Freud believed, the credibility of religion must be destroyed. It was, quite simply, the "enemy." "Of the three powers [art, philosophy, and religion] that may contest the very soil of science," he wrote, "religion alone is the serious enemy."[8] As his admiring biographer Peter Gay notes, "Freud in fact advertised his unbelief every time he could find, or make, an opportunity."[9]

Freud's major achievement, as he understood it, was to provide a complete "scientific" account of mental life. In doing so, he believed, he had offered a comprehensive alternative to the traditional religious view of the "soul." But psychoanalysis was more than a critique of religion; it was designed as a replacement. Freud's doctrines always had the character of a "substitute religion"—as Pfister himself complained in correspondence with Freud.[10] Moreover, it was a substitute religion with enormous popular appeal. As early as 1909, the "Viennese libertine" (as the *New York Times* dubbed Freud)[11] captured the American fancy when he paid his first visit to the United States. His audacious talk of childhood sexuality, incest, and the need to overcome repression of sexual urges tantalized the public imagination. Widely interpreted (or misinterpreted) as a call to personal sexual liberation, Freud's doctrines fed the loosening sexual prohibitions and rising divorce rates that characterized the racy pre-Depression era. By the 1920s, his psychoanalytic terminology—inferiority complex, sadism, masochism, Oedipus complex—was the stuff of cocktail party chitchat.[12] In the immediate post–World War II years, the influence of psychoanalytic thinking became even more pervasive as psychoanalytic institutes multiplied and the Freudian gospel spread to every level of American culture, from women's magazines to the highest reaches of academe. Benjamin Spock rewrote the rules of child rearing based on Freudian principles in a text that became the handbook of millions of parents. *Mademoiselle* instructed its readers on the ins and outs of "transference" and the Oedipus complex,[13] while Lionel Trilling, the country's most distinguished literary scholar, could intone: "The Freudian psychology is the only systematic account of the human mind which, in point of subtlety and complexity, of interest and tragic power, deserves to stand beside the chaotic mass of psychological insights which literature has accumulated through the centuries."[14]

Indeed, by the middle of the century, psychoanalysis—and psychotherapy generally—had achieved the status of a kind of "fifth estate" in society, an institution with prestige and power comparable to that of the media or the church. Psychiatrists and psychologists were modernity's new "wise men"—and women. Moreover, in the great rivalry between psychology and religion, psychology appeared to have the clear upper hand. Many mid-twentieth-century thinkers believed that the psychiatrist's couch was destined to replace the pulpit and the confessional as modern humanity's new source of moral guidance and spiritual solace. In 1966, the scholar Philip Rieff dubbed this phenomenon "the triumph of the therapeutic."[15]

Yet the last quarter of the twentieth century has not been kind to the psychoanalytic vision. Most significant has been the exposure of Freud's views of religion (not to mention a host of other matters)[16] as entirely fallacious. Ironically enough, scientific research in psychology over the past twenty-five years has demonstrated that, far from being a neurosis or source of neuroses as Freud and his disciples claimed, religious belief is one of the most consistent correlates of overall mental health and happiness. Study after study has shown a powerful relationship between religious belief and practice, on the one hand, and healthy behaviors with regard to such problems as suicide, alcohol and drug abuse, divorce, depression, even, perhaps surprisingly, levels of sexual satisfaction in marriage, on the other. In short, the empirical data run exactly contrary to the supposedly "scientific" consensus of the psychotherapeutic profession. The peculiarity of the situation is highlighted by David B. Larson, a former National Institutes of Health psychiatrist who has catalogued many of these studies:

> If a new health treatment were discovered that helped to reduce the rate of teenage suicide, prevent drug and alcohol abuse, improve treatment for depression, reduce recovery time from surgery, lower divorce rates and enhance a sense of well-being, one would think that every physician in the country would be scrambling to try it. Yet, what if critics denounced this treatment as harmful, despite research findings that showed it to be effective more than 80 percent of the time? Which would you be more ready to believe—the assertions of the critics based on their opinions or the results of the clinical trials based upon research?[17]

The "new health treatment" that Larson is talking about, of course, is religious faith. Numerous studies show that religious believers are far less likely than nonbelievers to commit suicide, abuse drugs or alcohol, experience debilitating stress, or get depressed or divorced.[18] Moreover, people of committed religious faith consistently report much higher levels of personal happiness and psychological well-being than do their agnostic or atheistic counterparts.[19]

To have overlooked such a powerful source of mental well-being—indeed, to have mistaken it for a form of mental *disorder*—cannot be counted a minor oversight in a discipline that nominated itself as the "science" of mental health. It shows to what degree the term "science" has been abused by the thinkers of modernity to mask what amounts to little more than a priori prejudice against the idea of God. In truth, there was nothing scientific at all about Freud's theory of religion: It was based on an imaginative misinterpretation of the then-prevalent ethnographic theories and has since been discredited.[20] Indeed, as numerous researchers have shown in recent years, there was little that was genuinely scientific about Freud's theories as a whole.[21] Yet the aura of "science" endowed Freud's doctrines with enormous legitimacy, sanctioning a host of experiments in personal and social behavior, many—as we shall see in a moment—with disastrous results.

THE FAITH FACTOR

At the root of modern psychology was a Faustian ambition: to replace the traditional religious understanding of the soul with a complete new mechanistic, "value-free" account of mental life based entirely on science. This ambition was announced as long ago as the seventeenth century by Thomas Hobbes—the first modern thinker to attempt to apply the methods of the new physical sciences to social and mental life. (Hobbes's denial of the soul won him wide condemnation as an atheist.)[22] Freud's comments on religion and science were merely an audacious re-statement of this original modern and Enlightenment theme.[23] But as the twentieth century winds to a close, the modern secular psychological paradigm is in a state of intellectual collapse. Far from confirming the various modernist theories of mental life, decades of research and clinical practice have in fact demonstrated, again and again, the impossibility of formulating a coherent view of human life absent the moral and religious horizon. Slowly but surely, modern psychology is belatedly rediscovering the soul.

Take the research on religious belief itself. The verdict here is overwhelming. It is difficult to find a more consistent correlative of mental health, or a better insurance against self-destructive behaviors, than a strong religious faith. A sample of the findings:

Suicide. A large-scale 1972 study found that persons who did not attend church were *four times as likely* to commit suicide than were frequent church attenders. A review of twelve studies of the relationship between religious commitment and suicide found a negative correlation in all twelve cases. Lack of church attendance has been found to be the single best predictor of suicide rates, better even than unemployment.[24]

Drug Abuse. Numerous studies have found an inverse correlation between religious commitment and abuse of drugs. One survey of nearly 14,000 youths found that substance abuse varied in direct proportion to strength of religious commitment, with the most conservative religious youths abusing the least. The authors concluded that "importance of religion" was the single best predictor of substance abuse patterns.[25]

Alcohol Abuse. Several studies have found that alcohol abuse is highest among those with little or no religious commitment. One study found that nearly 90 percent of alcoholics had lost interest in religion in youth, while among the nonalcoholic control group 48 percent reported an increase in religious commitment in adulthood and 32 percent reported no change.[26]

Depression and Stress. Several studies have found that high levels of religious commitment correlate with lower levels of depression, lower levels of stress, and greater ability to cope with stress. Religious people recover from surgery more quickly than do their atheistic and agnostic counterparts.[27]

Divorce. A number of studies have found a strong inverse correlation between church attendance and divorce. Church attendance also correlates strongly with the expressed willingness of a partner to marry the same spouse again—a measure of marital satisfaction.[28]

Marital and Sexual Satisfaction. A 1978 study found that church attendance predicted marital satisfaction better than any other single variable. Couples in long-lasting marriages who were surveyed in another study listed religion as one of the most important "prescriptions" of a happy marriage. *Most strikingly, an analysis of data from a massive survey of* Redbook *magazine readers in the 1970s found that "very religious women report greater happiness and satisfaction with marital sex than either moderately religious or nonreligious women."*[29] So religious people even seem to enjoy better marital sex!

Overall Happiness and Psychological Well-Being. Strong religious believers consistently report greater overall happiness and satisfaction with life. In one Gallup survey, respondents with a strong religious commitment—who agreed that "My religious faith is the most important influence in my life"—were *twice* as likely as those with minimal spiritual commitment to describe themselves as "very happy."[30]

To be sure, there are exceptions to every rule, and one can no doubt find cases where extreme religious views are bound up in psychopathologies. But the statistics make a powerful statement about the typical human condition. In short, if religion is an "obsessional neurosis," we should all hope to be "neurotic" in this way.

VALUE-FREE LIVING

Interestingly, the data correlating religious commitment with mental well-being is mirrored by growing evidence of a powerful relationship between licentious conduct and unhappiness, or what we might call, in plainer language, sin and misery. One of the most striking examples comes from *The New Harvard Guide to Psychiatry* (hardly a religious text), published in 1988. In a chapter on the adolescent, the editor, a Harvard Medical School psychiatry professor, detailed some of the pernicious psychological and health consequences of the sexual revolution and youth promiscuity of the 1960s, 1970s, and 1980s:

> Many who have worked closely with adolescents over the past decade have realized that the new sexual freedom has by no means led to greater pleasures, freedom, and openness; more meaningful relationship between the sexes; or exhilarating relief from stifling inhibitions. Clinical experience has shown that the new permissiveness has often led to empty

relationships, feelings of self-contempt and worthlessness, an epidemic of venereal disease, and a rapid increase in unwanted pregnancies. Clinicians working with college students began commenting on these effects as early as 20 years ago. They noted that students caught up in this new sexual freedom found it "unsatisfying and meaningless." . . . A more recent study of normal college students (those not under the care of a psychiatrist) found that, although their sexual behavior by and large appeared to be a desperate attempt to overcome a profound sense of loneliness, they described their sexual relationships as less than satisfactory and as providing little of the emotional closeness they desired. . . . They described pervasive feelings of guilt and haunting concerns that they were using others and being used as "sexual objects."[31]

The author went on to quote Freud on the inadvisability of unrestricted sexual freedom. (Of course, while Freud was on record opposing promiscuity, his early theory of repressed sexual urges or the "dammed-up libido" made a major contribution to the transformation in Western sexual mores.)[32] The author then commented on the trend toward religious revival among youth:

The disillusionment of late adolescence with this sphere of their lives as well as with drugs has contributed to the recent religious preoccupation among youth, especially the trend toward traditional religious faith. Although the basic Judeo-Christian morality conflicts strongly with their past behavior and current mores, they find the clear-cut boundaries it imposes less confusing than no boundaries at all and more helpful in relating to members of the opposite sex as "persons rather than sexual objects."[33]

Some of the clearest evidence that has been accumulated along these lines comes in the field of divorce. Many, though not all, religions place prohibitions on divorce (Jesus in the New Testament texts is particularly emphatic on this theme). Such prohibitions turn out to have not merely a spiritual, but also a strong public health, justification. Basically, the research shows that divorced and separated people are more likely than the general population to suffer serious physical and mental health problems and are at significantly higher risk for alcohol abuse, premature death, and suicide. (One could contemplate the posting of one of those famous "Surgeon General's Warnings" over the doors of divorce courts.) This is to say nothing of the harmful consequences for children, extending from poorer school performance to higher rates of juvenile delinquency and teen suicide among youths from broken homes—all of which have been amply documented.[34]

In short, the burden of both clinical experience and the research data suggests that among the most important determinants of human happiness and psychological well-being are our spiritual beliefs and moral choices. At least in the aggregate, people who have strong religious faith and attempt to live by its principles will tend to be much happier and lead far more productive lives than people who don't. This is not to deny the importance of other factors in making for mental stability or to argue that psychotherapy cannot be of great use to individuals in healing the wounds of their past. But it does suggest the inutility of approaches to therapy that ignore the spiritual dimension of human existence or that have nothing to say about right or wrong.

It is precisely the inability to speak to the last issue that has helped spell the catastrophic decline in the reputation of traditional psychoanalysis in recent years. The problem was dramatically exposed during the famous Woody Allen–Mia Farrow child custody case in the early 1990s. Allen had spent years in psychoanalysis, and a number of psychiatrists testified in the case. Psychiatrist William Doherty, who has written on the issue of psychiatry and moral responsibility, provides an excellent commentary on the issue:

> A prominent issue was Allen's fitness as parent, given his secret affair with Farrow's 19-year-old daughter. As in most child custody disputes, no one came out unscathed, least of all the therapists who testified as expert witnesses. When questioned about whether they thought it was wrong for Allen to have a secret affair with his lover's daughter, the therapists all demurred from making evaluative judgments. They used language reminiscent of the Watergate hearings: Mr. Allen "may have made an error in judgment," "a mistake given the circumstances," and—my personal favorite—the situation was a reflection of "the postmodern family." Finally, in a moment of exasperation after trying unsuccessfully to get any expert witness to break out of morally neutral therapeutic discourse, the judge angrily cut off one with these words: "I find it extraordinary the words that therapists use who come here, and they can say 'bad judgment' or 'lack of judgment.' But isn't there something stronger? You went through the 'postmodern structure of the family' and types of relationships. We're not at the point of sleeping with our children's sisters. What does it mean?"[35]

The Allen case vividly illustrated the hazards of "value-free" living—and of a "substitute religion" that sanctions such a lifestyle.

SPIRITUAL GROWTH

Far from replacing religion, modern psychology at the close of the twentieth century seems to be reacquainting itself with religion—reimporting into psychological theory many of the religious ideas and moral categories that were once banished as vestiges of an obsolete, unscientific worldview. Of course, there always was an alternative strand of thinking among psychological theorists that was far less hostile to religion than Freud was. Jung's differences with his former mentor on this issue are well known. "Among all my patients in the second half of my life," Jung observed in 1932, ". . . there has not been one whose problem in the last resort was not that of finding a religious outlook on life. It is safe to say that every one of them fell ill because he had lost that which the living religions of every age have given their followers and none of them has been really healed who did not regain his religious outlook."[36] Jung played an indirect role in the founding of Alcoholics Anonymous, in which the acknowledgment of a "Higher Power" forms a central plank of this most famously successful treatment for alcoholism.[37] Erich Fromm was an agnostic who took a much less critical view of religion and who absorbed important religious concepts into his theory of personality—notably the New Testament idea of *agape*, or unconditional love.[38] Viktor Frankl, a survivor of Auschwitz, formulated a brand of existential therapy that incorporated spiritual conceptions into therapy in a unique fashion. His *Man's Search for Meaning* was one of the century's more popular books.[39] During the 1970s, Abraham Maslow pioneered the psychological investigation of mystical or "peak" experiences—treating them not, as Freud would have done, as instances of "primary narcissism" but rather as manifestations of a higher form of consciousness.[40]

An important sign of change came with the publication of M. Scott Peck's *The Road Less Traveled: A New Psychology of Love, Traditional Values, and Spiritual Growth* in 1978.[41] Peck openly criticized his psychiatric colleagues for slighting religion and offered his own synthesis of religion and psychoanalysis, a new psychological approach that mixed talk of "repression" and "cathexis" with a stress on such traditional values as discipline, self-sacrifice, love, even "grace." Evidently, Peck's book struck a chord; it remained on the *New York Times* best-seller list for more than ten years. A second best-seller followed—*People of the Lie*, in which Peck made the case for a recovery of the category of "evil" in psychoanalytic discourse.[42] As the best-selling psychological text of the last quarter of the twentieth century, *The Road Less Traveled* altered the terms of public discourse about psychology and helped to shatter the taboo against religion that was once an integral part of psychoanalytic thinking.

The center of the old psychology-religion debate has been shifting and continues to shift. Increasingly, grass-roots therapists and popular writers on psychology are reintroducing religious ideas into therapy: The new literature on "forgiveness" is an interesting example.[43] Such a term would have had no place in the Freudian nomenclature. Yet a number of psychologists now argue that healing of such wounds as child abuse is impossible so long as the victim is unwilling to forgive. Books on "spiritually" based psychological approaches are so numerous today as to constitute a major trend in the discipline. A glance today at the psychology section of any bookstore will reveal scores of titles alluding to spiritual themes: "soul," "spiritual growth," "forgiveness," "love."

Moreover, an increasing number of psychologists and psychiatrists are beginning to acknowledge the data showing the strong positive link between religious commitment and mental health. "While Freud dismissed religion as little more than a neurotic illusion, the emerging wisdom in psychology is that at least some varieties of religious experience are beneficial for mental health," the *New York Times* reported in 1991. "The result is that growing numbers of psychologists are finding religion, if not in their personal lives, at least in their data. What was once, at best, an unfashionable topic in psychology has been born again as a respectable focus for scientific research."[44]

Side by side with these developments has come an institutional shift. Use of traditional psychoanalysis is declining, partly because of diminishing faith in its effectiveness, partly because insurers have become less willing to pay for the lengthy treatment it entails. Meanwhile, one of the greatest sources of growth in the mental health industry has come in so-called congregation-based and Christian counseling—church-sponsored and religiously oriented counseling centers that explicitly mix techniques from secular psychotherapy with religious themes. New Life, one of the largest organizations offering religiously oriented therapy, now operates some seventy clinics in fifty cities across the country.[45] The American Association of Christian Counselors, an organization of mostly evangelical Protestant therapists, grew from 751 members in 1991 to more than 14,000 in 1995. "Some of the most enthusiastic advocates of spiritually oriented counseling," writes psychologist Lewis Andrews, "are medical doctors and insurance officials who believe that religious faith helps many patients cope with life-threatening illnesses."[46]

In short, the mid-twentieth-century concern that modern psychology would supplant religion has not been borne out. What we see instead, on a variety of fronts, is the emergence of a postsecular synthesis—a new way of thinking about mental life that blends modern therapeutic insights and techniques with a reaffirmation of the moral and spiritual dimensions of human life.

THE RELIGIOUS DRIVE

Can modern psychology's late-twentieth-century rediscovery of religion be taken in any way as evidence for the validity of the broadly religious worldview or for the existence of God? It is indirect evidence of a sort, in the sense that the solution to the conundrum of mental health, stability, and happiness appears to lie beyond the reach of a purely materialistic or secular model of human consciousness. The effort to explain mental life, or devise a model of mental health, without reference to God was tried and failed. Of course Freud implicitly defined mental health, reasonably enough, as a state of mind free from "illusions," and one could argue that if religiously committed people report higher levels of psychological well-being, it is precisely because they *have* illusions. In essence, so the argument might run, religious believers are too naïve to understand how miserable life really is.

Interestingly, there is a growing body of research showing that certain kinds of illusions are in fact conducive to happiness and also—what is perhaps more puzzling—to physical health and career success. In particular, the "illusion" of optimism seems to be an important ingredient of a happy, healthy, and successful life. As psychologist Martin Seligman has shown, an individual's "explanatory style"—the way he or she interprets the events that occur in life and his or her expectations about the future—can profoundly affect levels of psychological and physical well-being as well as job and school performance. He has shown that pessimism—a pessimistic "explanatory style"— leads to greater levels of unhappiness and failure in life; indeed, it can actually cause depression. Tests designed to measure individuals' levels of optimism and pessimism are reliable predictors of job performance. In one survey of sales agents, for example, the top 10 percent on the optimistic scale sold 88 percent more than the 10 percent who scored most pessimistic.[47] Of course, one of the most profound and global sources of optimism is religious belief. (One recalls evangelist Billy Graham's response when a U.S. senator asked him whether he was an optimist or a pessimist. "I'm an optimist," he answered. ". . . I've read the last page of the Bible.")[48] "Organized religion," Seligman writes, "provides a belief that there is more good to life than meets the eye." Seligman sees clear psychological benefits in this sort of optimism, citing findings showing lower levels of depression among the religiously committed. He even speculates that the loss of religious belief in the 1960s was partly responsible for the dark mood and national disasters—from race riots to the Vietnam War to national disillusionment—of that era.[49]

Of course, the religious terms for optimism are *faith* and *hope*. It is more than a little ironic that after its long odyssey into the unconscious and its multiplication of dark modernistic concepts of mental life, modern psychology at the end of the twentieth century should have arrived at a formula for mental well-being and happiness hardly distinguishable from that of traditional religion—faith, hope, love, self-discipline, and a life lived in conformity with solid, traditional moral principles. This is by no means to discount what modern psychology has learned, through research and clinical experience, about the effect of childhood memory or mechanisms such as denial or repression. It is not to denigrate the effectiveness of psychotherapy or even the use of psychotropic drugs to address mental ailments. It is certainly not to argue that the adoption of a religious worldview spells an instant end to one's psychological troubles or to deny that obsessive and extreme religious views can be pathological. But it is to say that modern psychology's outright rejection of God was an intellectual error even within the terms of the discipline and that views of the nature of human consciousness derived from modern psychology and from religious revelation have tended to converge rather diverge over the past twenty years.

In effect, at the end of the twentieth century, modern psychology has found what we might call telltale signs of the soul. Indeed, the burden of the research would invite the speculation that the human mind is in some sense *designed* to require faith—that the religious "drive" or hunger is at least as powerful as any other, that the human mind does not find itself at rest until it acknowledges and develops a relationship with the god-head. Of course, religious people would not find this notion surprising—even though for decades modern psychology tried to argue otherwise. Such a train of thought might also form the beginnings of a potentially promising theodicy, or an explana-tion of the "problem of evil." For if "this world" holds out many pleasures, it also delivers more than enough pain to com-pel the mind to seek its ultimate source of hope beyond this world. Those who confine their search for happiness to the glo-ries and pleasures of the secular or material world, who live in denial of the godhead, will, as a practical matter, encounter much more mental tension (and, as the research shows, will be far more likely to shipwreck on mental illness, drugs, or alcohol) than will those who treat the present life as a spiritual journey—a teaching that, not coincidentally, virtually all the major religious traditions—from Judaism and Christianity to Islam, Buddhism, and Hinduism—share.

Moreover, modern research tends to bear out the ob-servation that sin breeds misery. It turns out that the Ten Commandments—or the basic moral law as expressed by any of the major religions—are not just an arbitrary set of divinely ordained taboos or a path to a happy afterlife; they are also a very reliable guide to happiness and health in this world. As a child, one is forced, with a naïveté similar to the biblical Adam's, to take this on faith. But one cannot reach a certain age without observing the enormous disruption and pain that serious breaches of the moral law cause even in the life of the "sinner." Adultery is a prominent example. Who has not known individuals who have ruined their lives almost beyond repair by yielding to a stupid temptation or placing the gratifi-cation of the moment ahead of their responsibilities to those whom they love? Yet even such failings and the sorrows that follow tend, in the logic of human mental life, to drive many such individuals back, eventually, to God. Countless are the cases where the descent to despair via alcohol, drugs, sex addiction, or some other path was the prelude to a recovery of faith: The founder of Alcoholics Anonymous, Bill W., is a well-known example. From the depths of an alcoholic despair, praying for the first time in many years, he had, by his own report, a mystical experience that led him not only to stop drinking but also to go on later to found AA.[50] In effect, one could argue, the world is designed to present the mind with a fundamental moral choice as well as a dilemma whose only solution lies in an acknowledgment of, and encounter with, God. But we are venturing into the terrain of the theologians.

Even if we set aside the issue of what the structure of the human psyche may or may not imply about the existence of God, the findings of modern psychological research introduce an important change in the terms of the age-old debate between believers and atheists. In particular, it leads to a reevaluation of Pascal's famous "wager." Responding to the first generation of modern atheistic rationalists in the seventeenth century, the mathematician and philosopher Blaise Pascal offered an interesting "thought experiment" concerning religious belief. He conceived of the issue as a bet or wager. His reasoning was as follows: Revelation teaches that God rewards faithful believers with eternal happiness and that those who reject God suffer eternal torment after death. There is no way for reason, Pascal conceded to his contemporaries, to know whether revelation's claim is true. But we may consider our life as a wager (one that, in the nature of things, we can't avoid). If we bet against God, and revelation proves to be true, we will suffer eternal torment. If we bet for God, and revelation proves to have been an illusion, we lose nothing, for we shall cease to exist at death in any case.

Of course, the touchy issue here concerns what those who opt for belief must sacrifice in this life: Revelation teaches that they must, in Pascal's words, "curtail" their "passions." Pascal tried to minimize this sacrifice by pointing to the purely rational benefits of a life lived in conformity with the moral law. "Now, what harm will you come by," he wrote, "in making this choice? You will be faithful, honest, humble, grateful, generous, a sincere friend, truthful. Certainly, you will not enjoy those pernicious delights—glory and luxury; but will you not experience others?"[51] The atheist and agnostic suspicion has always been that Pascal had soft-pedaled the sacrifice end of the bargain. In giving up the pleasures and glories that religion teaches us to forgo, so the atheist argument has run, we are indeed sacrificing much. (Nietzsche, in his antireligious diatribes, made a particular point of emphasizing this, preaching the theoretical superiority of the life based on gratification of violent and erotic instincts, the "nobility" of the "barbarian"—a major reason that the Nazis found certain passages of his books so congenial.)[52] But modern research in psychology makes clear that the morally unrestrained life is not worth living. The crowning irony is this: Even if their beliefs were to be proved illusions, religiously committed people lead happier and healthier lives, as numerous studies show.

But the larger point to recognize is that the modern secular psychological paradigm—the effort to give a complete account of the workings of the human mind without reference to God or spirit—has crumbled. Modernity failed to achieve its ambition of a comprehensive, materialistic alternative to the religious understanding of the human condition. A purely secular view of human mental life has been shown to fail not just at the theoretical, but also at the practical, level. The last thing Freud would have predicted as the outcome of more than a half century's scientific psychological research and therapeutic experience was the rediscovery of the soul.

three

Faith
and the
Physicians

Alongside the findings from psychology, a growing body of evidence from medical research shows a strong positive link between religious commitment and physical health. At first glance, this should not be surprising, given what medicine has learned in recent years about the connection between illness and stress. If religion is a stress-reducer—and the data suggest overwhelmingly that it can be a powerful one—then we should expect religiously committed people, on average, to have lower rates of disease. One does not have to invoke divine intervention to explain this outcome. Certainly, it is unnecessary to raise the suggestion, as a recent *Time* cover story on the subject did, that when it comes to health, "the faithful actually have God on their side."[1] Rather, the argument takes place on a different plane: Just as the anthropic principle reveals a physical universe seemingly designed expressly for human life, so what we have learned from psychology and medicine in recent years increasingly points to a mind and body designed for religious faith. The religious drive or hunger appears to be so profound as to have major measurable physiological consequences. Moreover, there is abundant empirical evidence for the beneficial health effects of certain religious states of consciousness—meditative or prayerful states of mind. In short, medicine, too, is on the verge of a postsecular revolution. It is rediscovering the soul. As Harvard Medical School associate professor of medicine Herbert Benson puts it, contemporary medical research is showing that the human mind and body are "wired for God."[2]

A HEALTHY FAITH

The epidemiological evidence for the health benefits of religious belief and commitment, compiled by David B. Larson and his team at the National Institute for Healthcare Research, is impressive. Some examples:

- A major 1972 study examined death from various causes among adults in Washington County, Maryland, in relation to church attendance. Factors such as smoking, socioeconomic status, and water hardness were controlled for statistically. Findings were as follows: (1) Risk of arteriosclerotic heart disease for men who attended church frequently was just *60 percent* of that for men who were infrequent church attenders. (2) Among women, risk of dying from arteriosclerotic heart disease, pulmonary emphysema, and suicide was *twice* as high among infrequent as among frequent church attenders. (3) Women who attended church infrequently were four times as likely as frequent church attenders to die from cirrhosis of the liver (a finding that may relate to the data showing much lower levels of alcohol abuse among the religiously committed).[3]

- Blood pressure has been shown to be strongly correlated with religious commitment and church attendance. Religiously committed people and frequent church attenders have, on average, significantly lower blood pressure than do the religiously noncommitted and those who attend church infrequently. A 1989 study of rural men by Larson and others found that those who counted religion as very important in their lives and attended church frequently had, on average, diastolic pressure levels nearly 5 millimeters lower than did those who counted religion as unimportant and attended church infrequently. The effects were so profound as to suggest a public health justification for encouraging more frequent church attendance, since a reduction in blood pressure by as little as 2 to 4 millimeters in a population could bring a 10 to 20 percent decline in cardiovascular disease.[4]

- The most startling finding concerned smokers: (1) Smokers who ranked religion as very important in their lives were *over seven times less likely* to have abnormal diastolic pressure readings than were those who did not. (2) Smokers who attended church frequently were *four times less likely* to have abnormal diastolic pressure readings than were infrequent church attenders.[5]

- A comprehensive 1987 review of nearly 250 epidemiological studies found positive associations between religious affiliation and physical health.[6]
- A 1991 analysis of polling data from the National Opinion Research Center, which included questions on
  health and levels of religious commitment, found that
  levels of religious commitment as measured by self-
  reported frequency of church attendance and frequency
  of prayer correlated significantly with self-reported
  health status, regardless of the respondent's age. [7]

WIRED FOR PRAYER

Some of the most interesting findings to emerge from this
new "postsecular" research concern the benefits of prayer.
Prayer, of course, had no place in the Freudian paradigm. It
is by and large not something that takes place in the modern physician's consulting room. (Medical doctors, like their
counterparts in psychiatry and clinical psychology, are much
more likely to identify themselves as atheists or agnostics than
is the general population—though levels of unbelief among
physicians treating the body do not match levels among those
who purport to treat the soul. A 1991 survey of family
practice physicians in Vermont, for example, found that only
64 percent of the doctors believed in God—in contrast to 91
percent of their patients.)[8] Yet opinion data show that prayer
plays an important role in the lives of the vast majority of
Americans. Various polls have indicated that over 90 percent
of women and 85 percent of men pray. Over three-quarters of
Americans pray at least once a week, and nearly 60 percent
pray once a day. Paradoxically, even among the 13 percent of

the population who describe themselves as atheists or agnostics, one in five reports praying daily.[9] And in one Gallup survey sponsored by *Life* magazine, 95 percent responded "yes" to the question, "Have your prayers ever been answered?"[10]

Are the 95 percent of us who believe our prayers have on occasion been answered suffering from a collective delusion? If so, medical research shows it is one of the more beneficial delusions a person could have. Prayer has been shown to have enormous benefits, on both a macro and a micro scale. That is, opinion surveys consistently show a strong powerful correlation between frequent prayer and self-reported well-being. And laboratory research has revealed a connection between certain prayerful or meditative states and measurable improvements in physiological indicators and overall health.

One of the most sophisticated studies of religious commitment, prayer, and well-being was undertaken by M. M. Poloma and B. F. Pendleton in the early 1990s. These researchers added several questions to a large ongoing study of a random sample of residents of Akron, Ohio. They examined a number of different measures of religious commitment, including, among other things, frequency of church attendance, church membership, and frequency of prayer. They also divided prayer into types: colloquial ("How often do you ask God to provide guidance in making decisions?"), petitional ("How often do you ask God for material things that you need?"), ritual ("How often do you read from a book of prayer?"), and meditative ("How often do you spend time just 'feeling' or being in the presence of God?"). Nearly all the indicators of religious commitment, including frequency of prayer, correlated with well-being on various axes. But they also found an interesting distinction between types of prayer.

Exclusive use of ritual prayer and petitional prayer—in this case focused on "material things"—correlated with negative effects. (One is reminded of that amusing old Janis Joplin song: "O Lord, won't you buy me a Mercedes Benz!") Colloquial prayer correlated highest with life satisfaction, and meditative prayer with religious satisfaction and "existential well-being."[11]

In the late 1960s, Dr. Herbert Benson, associate professor of medicine at Harvard Medical School, undertook a series of studies of people practicing transcendental meditation. He found that meditation leaves a unique medical footprint—unlike that, say, of other forms of relaxation or of sleep (though somewhat closer to hypnosis). Metabolic rates of meditators, as measured by oxygen consumption, are rapidly lowered—more sharply and more deeply than would occur in sleep. Levels of blood lactate drop significantly over the course of the meditation (high levels are associated with high anxiety). Brain alpha wave activity—usually associated with feelings of well-being—increase. Moreover, meditators enjoy long-term health benefits. In his first set of studies, Benson established a link between daily meditation and lowered blood pressure levels. There was a less certain link with a drop in drug use, including smoking, among meditators. (These findings were reported in his best-selling 1975 book, *The Relaxation Response*.)[12] Since then, he and his team of researchers (now at the Mind/Body Institute at the Deaconess Hospital in Boston) have documented a long list of dramatic, life-improving effects on an impressive range of ailments (though, it should be pointed out, practice of the "relaxation response," as Benson calls it, was normally combined with a regimen that included nutrition, exercise, and other stress-management strategies). Significant improvements were achieved not only in hypertension, but also in chronic pain, insomnia, cardiac arrhythmia, cancer, AIDS, and a host of other diseases. Meditation appeared to have positive effects even on infertility. Remarkably, "thirty-six percent of women with unexplained infertility became pregnant within six months of completing the program."[13]

It should be emphasized that Benson did his best to present his regimen in a nondenominational and even nonreligious fashion. He permitted patients to choose any word or phrase as a meditative focus—or what the yogis call a "mantra." Catholics might repeat in their minds "Lord Jesus Christ, have mercy on me" or "Hail Mary, full of grace," while Protestants might repeat "Our Father, Who art in Heaven" or "The Lord is my Shepherd," and Jews might choose "Sh'ma Yisroel" or "Shalom." But there were also secular focus words for non-believers: "one," "ocean," "love," "peace," "calm," "relax." Interestingly, however, 80 percent of patients chose a religious focus; and 25 percent, regardless of whether they were secular or religious, reported greater feeling of spirituality as a result of meditation.[14] (Hollywood screenwriter and producer Marty Kaplan's story is interesting and illustrative in this regard. A *summa cum laude* graduate of Harvard in biology and a staunch agnostic, he took up meditation independently to cure his habit of grinding his teeth and rediscovered God in the process—as he wrote in *Time* magazine.)[15]

DEEPER INTO PARADOX

Benson is a careful scientist, and he relates the health benefits of religious commitment to the well-documented "placebo effect" in medicine; attempting to broaden the principle, he calls this effect "remembered wellness."[16] Enormous amounts of evidence demonstrate that if patients believe they are receiving an effective treatment—even if that treatment is a sugar pill—they will often get better. Additional evidence suggests that the physician's belief concerning the efficacy of a particular treatment can affect its outcome.[17] But Benson contends that there is something uniquely powerful and overarching about faith in God or in some form of transcendent reality in calming the mind, enhancing hope, and even increasing the efficacy of particular medical treatments: "I have found that faith quiets the mind like no other form of belief."[18] Significantly, he discovered that practice of the relaxation response itself worked best when it was supported by a faith-filled worldview:

> . . . It became clear that a person's religious convictions or life philosophy enhanced the average effects of the relaxation response in three ways: (1) People who chose an appropriate focus, that which draws upon their deepest philosophic or religious convictions, were more apt to adhere to the elicitation routine, looking forward to it and enjoying it; (2) Affirmative beliefs of any kind brought forth remembered wellness, reviving top-down nerve-cell-firing patterns in the brain that were associated with wellness; (3) When present, faith in an eternal or life-transcending force seemed to make the fullest use of remembered wellness because it is a supremely soothing belief, disconnecting unhealthy logic and worries.[19]

This is an important finding. Remember that Benson tried to divorce meditative techniques from religious content or meaning. Indeed, his best-selling 1975 book, *The Relaxation*

Response, presented the technique in an entirely secular spirit (I remember being struck by this when I read the book, as an atheist, years ago). But now we find that not only did the vast majority of his patients choose a religious focus or mantra, but also the technique itself worked best when underpinned by genuine faith on the patient's part. One suspects that there may be more to this phenomenon than simply the "calming" effect of religious belief. That is, the mind's ability to tap into the healing power of the meditative regimen is closely connected to its willingness to believe, to paraphrase Gertrude Stein, that there's a There there. Is this simply because of the way the brain is structured? Or does meditation—an ancient technique, after all a form of prayer, explicitly designed by religious seers to achieve spiritual closeness with the Deity or Absolute—only work completely when it is used for what it was designed to do? Further, we are presented with a mystery. Why in principle should the human brain be structured in such a way that a spiritual technique, a form of *prayer*, would bring not just peace of mind, but also measurable health benefits, sometimes seeming to verge on the miraculous, and why would this spiritual technique work best when combined with sincere *faith*?

True to the spirit of a scientist, Benson climbs to the very threshold of faith without being willing to cross it. He goes so far as to argue that the spiritual drive is absolutely fundamental to human physiology, that human beings are, as he puts it, "wired for God." But he chooses to see this as a purely biological adaptation, a "primal motive" or "survival instinct," hypothesizing that the human mind had to construct a God to cope with the rigors of its natural environment in the early stages of human evolution. He remains, at least by his own account, agnostic on the question of whether we seek God because the universe, and we, have been deliberately designed to do so—though his agnosticism amounts to a de facto temperamental scientific preference for a purely biological or evolutionary explanation for the phenomenon, should one be found:

> I believe that this is a proverbial chicken-or-egg question, and that it will be impossible for science to say which came first—the animal or the soul, man or the concept of God, a life in which faith became a survival strategy or the genes that made life and faith possible. Despite science's unceasing attempts to quiet it, the Mystery of our existence reverberates.
>
> But my scientific journey has led me to what I believe is a more important point, at least for my purposes as a physician. It does not matter which came first—God or the belief in God. The data I have presented is that affirmative beliefs and hopes are very therapeutic, and that faith in God, in particular, has many positive effects on health.[20]

Fair enough.

But when we consider Benson's new discoveries in light of the history of the modern evolutionary explanation for religious belief, such a hypothesis begins to look strangely forced. The notion that belief in God arose as the mind's defense mechanism in the face of primitive humanity's early struggle against nature was, in a sense, *the* modern scientific and atheistic explanation for religious belief. It was precisely this notion that Freud invoked in dismissing religion as an "infantile" illusion. But Benson's research—along with that of Larson and others—has complicated the picture enormously. For if this is an illusion, it is, first of all, *not* a harmful one, as Freud and the moderns taught. On the contrary, it is mentally beneficial. It is also, more puzzlingly, *physically* beneficial. And strangest of all, by deliberately *inter-acting* with this Illusion in a sincere spirit, through meditative prayer, one can create improvements in symptoms of disease that otherwise cannot be medically explained.

If this is merely a "survival strategy" or a defense mechanism, it is one of extraordinary complexity. In light of our new, expanded knowledge of this phenomenon, are we really prepared to argue that mere evolution—blind, chance mechanisms—brought about the creation of an illusory God to whom human beings could *pray* and receive, as *a result of this prayerful exercise*, remission in disease symptoms (such as infertility) that could not be relieved by other available medical means? Are we really supposed to believe that this is some sort of massive coincidence, the accidental by-product of processes that were dictated by purely materialistic, mechanistic forces churning blindly over time—which human beings in their benighted primitivism have foolishly mistaken across the centuries for God? And why, then, should *failure* to believe this particular illusion have physiological and psychological penalties—in the form, for example, of a greater risk for high blood pressure and death from heart attack or a greater susceptibility to such behaviors as drug abuse and suicide? If this were an illusion, it would be natural to think, as Freud did, that it is a problem and that it should be curable. But the opposite is the case: "Curing" the mind of this illusion places the body and mind at increased risk of disease, for which the Illusion itself can be a cure! As our scientific knowledge of these phenomena has deepened, the standard, modern atheistic explanation for them is driven further and further into paradox, almost to the point of absurdity.

RELIGION VERSUS MAGIC

There is another, far less conclusive, strand of research on prayer and disease that has tried to measure the effects of so-called "intercessory" prayer. This is a more daring enterprise: attempting to measure the effect of prayer not simply on the health of one who prays, but also on the health of others. In one 1969 triple-blind study, a prayer intervention group prayed for ten children with leukemia (the children were not aware they were being prayed for); another eight children served as a control group, for which the intervention group did not pray. (A number of critics have raised ethical issues about such studies, with reason.) After a fifteen-month period, seven out of ten children in the prayer group were alive; only two of the eight in the control group were alive. The point was to determine whether intercessory prayer could affect disease; however, critics point out that the sample was far too small to draw any conclusions.[21] A 1965 study similarly compared results for a prayer group and control group of patients suffering from "chronic stationary or progressively deteriorating psychological or rheumatic disease." Various clinical indicators were used to measure progress of the disease. No significant difference in outcome was detected between the two groups.[22]

The most widely publicized such double-blind study was undertaken by cardiologist Randolph Byrd, himself a believing Christian, at San Francisco General Hospital in the 1980s. Byrd's sample was sufficiently large: 393 coronary care patients. Of these, 192 were prayed for by prayer groups (comprising self-described "born-again" Catholics and Protestants of a devotional bent whom Byrd recruited for the purpose). The 201 patients in the control group were not prayed for.

The difference in outcome for the two groups was significant. Neither patient group had knowledge of the experiment. The group prayed for had fewer cases of congestive heart failure and cardiopulmonary arrest, as well as fewer cases of pneumonia. They also used diuretics and antibiotics less. The findings seemed impressive at first glance—wire services across the country headlined the story—but on careful examination, the study proved to be flawed because of too many uncontrolled factors and unknowns. First, the habits of the doctors treating the various patients were not controlled for. This raises questions about the findings regarding medication. Some physicians are quick to prescribe such medicines as antibiotics and diuretics, others slow to do so. Then there was the more fundamental problem of putting "prayer" itself in this fashion under the scientific microscope. Presumably, some of the patients in the control group had relatives and friends praying for them. Indeed, one would expect the majority of people in coronary care units to have people praying quite earnestly for them. Why should the prayers of the control group's relatives not have been "heard," while the prayers of the strangers in Byrd's recruited prayer groups were? Were the latter prayers "better," even though they came from strangers who did not know the patients? How earnestly did the prayer groups pray, and for that matter did they pray at all?[23] Byrd's was an ingeniously and carefully structured study. But as is clear, one sails quickly off the scientific deep end in this kind of research.

Significantly, no one has yet been able to replicate Byrd's findings. Other, similar studies are in progress.[24] Without prejudging the outcome of such research, one is inclined to raise questions about its underlying assumptions. First, while double-blind studies can capture a great deal, there are realities—and not just transcendental ones—beyond the reach of the scientific method. Second, the understanding of prayer underlying such studies seems overly mechanical. Indeed, it points to one of the real hazards of the postsecular revolution in medicine and the new discovery of "spiritual healing."

There is a kind of relentlessly utilitarian bent to the American mind that is prepared to reduce everything in life to a tool or a commodity. Spirituality is no exception. Think about it for a moment. Over the course of centuries, countless children have prayed earnestly over sick parents—and for that matter parents over sick children—who, despite countless, earnest prayers, have died. To date, none of us have escaped that particular earthly fate. Precious few of us escape illness over the course of a long life. Statistics show that religious people are, on average, physically and mentally healthier than their atheistic or agnostic counterparts, and that is well and good. Nevertheless, they do get sick, and they do die.

The notion that spiritual forces can be invoked at will to change the material conditions of our lives, or those of others, properly belongs not to religion or to genuine spirituality as it has been understood by mankind's greatest religious teachers, but rather to magic. It is not accidental that one of the most important phrases in Christian prayer is "Thy will be done." The Hebrew Bible and the New Testament alike emphasize over and over again that true prayer, and true spirituality, lies in submitting the human to the divine will, and not the reverse. They also stress that the divine plan is not necessarily the human plan. "'For my thoughts are not your thoughts, Neither are your ways My ways,' declares the Lord" (Isaiah 55:8).[25] Islam, Buddhism, and Hinduism likewise agree in their emphasis on *acceptance* of the suffering that life metes out as one of the most fundamental ingredients of true spirituality—and one of the most important spiritual lessons to be learned in an earthly life. The prayerful and meditative states taught by the world's great religions and the world's great mystics are states of humble acceptance.

It is worth remembering that religion, or true spirituality, does not promise exemption from suffering; on the contrary, it teaches the inevitability of suffering and even the necessity of suffering as a means of strengthening the soul and turning it from this world toward God. The prayerful or meditative states and outlooks that Benson finds so beneficial to health have precisely this character of acceptance. The great religions teach that one gains—here or hereafter—by sincerely giving up, by submitting to the divine will. "For whoever wishes to save his life will lose it; but whoever loses his life for My sake will find it" (Matthew 16:25).

Some New Age approaches to spirituality, in particular, part ways with religion and true spirituality in favor of magic. The various claims that certain spiritual practices can halt the aging process, extend one's life span by many decades, or for that matter generate massive personal wealth—the well-grounded religious mind recognizes these as temptation in its classic form. They are not spirituality, but the parody of spirituality. They resemble one of those pernicious artificial chemical molecules that, mimicking a natural ingredient of the body, bonds with a living cell, weakening it, even rendering it cancerous. Magic consists of using the tools of the other world to achieve the goals of this one, rather than vice versa. That certain authors garner vast revenues by peddling such extravagant materialistic promises to the public in the name of spirituality should not be surprising, since the market for snake oil has always been bullish. But drinking snake oil usually does no good and often does harm. False promises such as these can be both a spiritual diversion and a hazard to one's health. Moreover, they encourage what psychologists call "magical thinking." It is absurd to get to the stage where one views the catching of a common cold or a sore throat as the sign of a major spiritual failing—a syndrome that has been almost proverbially common in New Age circles—or where one believes one can control health symptoms at will. (Of course, even our secular framework sometimes leads to this kind of thinking. Now that we know the link between colds and stress, we are sometimes inclined to seek out a psychological source for our sniffles.) Colds—and, for that matter, stress—are a part of life, as is much more profound pain and suffering, and normal maturity, to say nothing of "spiritual growth," entails accepting this.

TOWARD POSTSECULAR MEDICINE?

Nonetheless, contemporary medicine is clearly moving in the direction of acknowledging dimensions of healing beyond the purely material. In December 1995, the Harvard Medical School held its first conference on spirituality and healing in medicine, in cooperation with Benson's Mind/Body Institute at Deaconess Hospital. It featured a mix of prominent physicians and theologians.[26] One sign of increasing official recognition of the spiritual dimension of healing was the creation by Congress of an Office of Alternative Medicine (OAM) at the National Institutes of Health in 1991. "Alternative medicine" covers a wide range of treatments from chiropractic medicine to herbal treatments to changes in lifestyle and nutritional habits. But part of the OAM's mandate is to examine "mind-body" effects, which provides an official umbrella and funding for what can only be called postsecular medical research.[27] Exploration of this area is still in its infancy, but one suspects that with time greater research attention will be devoted to this field.

A related and important issue concerns religion and spirituality as subjects in medical education and training. Traditionally, the perspective underlying the training of medical and mental health professionals has been relentlessly secular—perhaps appropriately so in the case of physicians, since one desires to train doctors and not shamans or medicine men! Still, as David Larson argues, there are good reasons for including a component in medical education that covers issues of religion and spirituality as they relate to health. First, as we have seen, evidence shows that "the faith factor" can make important contributions to health and healing. Second, most patients whom doctors see believe that they have souls as well as bodies. Interestingly, a 1966 Time/CNN poll by Yankelovich Partners found that 64 percent of Americans believed "Doctors should join their patients in prayer if the patients request it." Only 27 percent disagreed.[28] Physicians, patients, and patients' families confront a host of life-and-death decisions together. Even if the physician is not a believer, a greater understanding of the role that religion may play in patients' lives and decisions would doubtless enhance mutual communication on these exceedingly difficult and often sorrowful dilemmas.

Larson's National Institute for Healthcare Research has developed materials for such courses. They are research-based and objective in character. The institute has also provided a small number of grants to medical schools willing to establish such a course. To date only a handful of medical schools have experimented with the approach. But there is every reason to suppose that as Larson's and Benson's work becomes more widely known, medical education will increasingly incorporate a postsecular component.

Perhaps the most difficult issue that physicians, patients, and patients' families face is death and dying. Over the past twenty years, thinking about the treatment of terminal illness has undergone a virtual revolution, thanks largely to the work of the Swiss-born physician Elisabeth Kübler-Ross. Her years of compassionate labor at the bedside of hundreds of terminally ill patients—summarized in her now canonical *On Death and Dying*[29] and other books—broke the taboo against talk of death that once prevailed in treatment of the terminally ill and also provided an analytical understanding of the stages of grief that both the dying and their loved ones must endure. In a society in which death increasingly had come to take place in the antiseptic environment of hospitals and in which an officially secular culture had robbed many people of the consoling framework that traditional religion once provided to the dying and their loved ones, Kübler-Ross's work could be considered an enormous contribution. Indeed, countless are the individuals and families who have benefited from Kübler-Ross's analytical road map to, and consoling yet realistic picture of, the process of death. But spending, as she did, so much time at the bedsides of the dying, Kübler-Ross stumbled on another phenomenon that, in a sense, defines the final frontier of postsecular research. Certain individuals, she found, had "died and made a comeback."[30] They described themselves floating out of their bodies and being greeted by a loved one or a religious figure who would aid their transition to a different realm. When they regained consciousness, they had vivid stories to tell of a world beyond death. This was not something that medical training or, for that matter, an orthodox religious background would prepare one for. (Kübler-Ross was raised Protestant, had married a Jew, and had at the time what she described as essentially indeterminate religious convictions.)[31] She was preparing to write up her findings on this issue when, coincidentally, a young philosophy professor turned psychiatrist at the University of Virginia, Raymond Moody, began a systematic investigation of such stories, spurred by the tale of a fellow psychiatrist, George Ritchie, who had had a particularly vivid such experience while suffering from pneumonia in the military during World War II. Moody published his preliminary findings in a 1975 book, *Life After Life*,[32] which quickly made its way to the best-seller lists (Kübler-Ross wrote a foreword to the volume).

Today the term *near-death experience* is a household word and the subject of numerous best-selling books. But simultaneous with the publication of this popular literature has been a scientific investigation of the phenomenon, and an accompanying debate, with interesting and puzzling results. These experiences turn out to be extraordinarily common. In the next chapter, we will take up the question: Can modern science satisfactorily account for the near-death experience through a purely physiological model, or does the near-death experience provide the first compelling scientific evidence for the independent existence of the soul?

four

Intimations

of

Immortality

Whten Raymond Moody published his famous 1975 book on the near-death experience (NDE), *Life After Life*,[1] it was greeted with a great deal of skepticism, not least in the medical and scientific communities. No one could deny that the story was deeply intriguing. Drawing on interviews with 150 subjects who claimed to have had such experiences, the book compiled firsthand accounts of a world beyond death. Subjects who had suffered a heart attack or some other physical catastrophe described "dying," floating outside of their bodies, and observing medical resuscitation procedures performed on them from a vantage point above the event. They described feelings of peace, well-being, and weightlessness and the ability to travel instantly via thought. Many reported whooshing rapidly through a dark tunnel toward a point of light. At the end of this tunnel, they encountered a heavenly landscape and a "Being of Light," whom many identified as Christ. Colors were unearthly and vivid. The light emanating from the Being was said to be many times brighter than anything they had ever seen—yet it did not hurt one's eyes.

Above all, the Being was said to convey a powerful, unearthly, unconditional love. Some of the experiencers reported having seen and communicated with relatives who had died. A few described an extended encounter with the Being of Light, a conversation and a "life review"—a detailed replay of their entire lives in three dimensions, which consisted of all their thoughts and actions as well as the effects of their thoughts and actions on others; during this "replay," the Being helped them understand what they had done right and what they had done wrong. All of this seemed remarkable—and utterly fantastic. It did not even conform that closely with orthodox religious teachings about heaven, hell, and the afterlife. Who could believe it?

One of the skeptics was Dr. Michael Sabom, then a first-year cardiologist at the University of Florida.[2] Sabom stumbled on Moody's book somewhat by happenstance a year after it had been published. His wife and he had just joined a local Methodist church. A psychiatric social worker from the university gave a talk on Moody's book during an adult Sunday school class. Others in the class were enthusiastic about the discussion, but Sabom was annoyed and unimpressed. "The kindest thing I could find to say at the moment," he wrote later, "was 'I don't believe it.'"[3] Though a churchgoer, Sabom considered himself first and foremost a scientist. "Early on in medical school, I strongly embraced [the] basic logic of the scientific method in relation to the diagnosis and treatment of disease." His concern was saving patients from death, not worrying about the afterlife. "I suppose if someone had asked me what I thought of death, I would have said that with death you are dead and that is the end of it. Although I had been raised in a churchgoing family, I had always tried to keep religious and scientific doctrines separate. For me at the time, Christian beliefs in life after death served the purpose of guiding proper worldly behavior and of relieving anxieties about death and dying, but such teachings remained subjective and unscientific."[4]

The psychiatric social worker pressed him to join her in a presentation about Moody's findings to a churchwide audience. He resisted at first but later reluctantly agreed. The two of them would try an experiment: Before the talk, each would try to find at least one patient who had had a near-death experience. If there were such people, it should not be difficult for Sabom or his colleague to locate one. Sabom was working with heart patients; the social worker was stationed in a kidney dialysis unit. Both groups had frequent brushes with death. He began asking around. The third patient he inquired of—a middle-aged woman from Tampa—"began describing the first near-death experience I had heard in my medical career."[5] Sarah, the social worker, similarly found a patient who reported an NDE.

They gave the talk. But Sabom remained skeptical and deeply dissatisfied with the unscientific, anecdotal nature of Moody's book. Most of the stories in *Life After Life* were recounted by people long after the events. No data were presented on the nature of the sample. Moreover, it was far from a random one: These people had come to Moody with their stories, sometimes following lectures he gave on NDEs. It was impossible to tell how many of Moody's 150 subjects had experienced the various aspects of the NDE—the tunnel, the Being of Light, the life review, and so forth. In addition, Moody provided no detail whatever on the individuals' medical conditions or treatment at the time of the NDE. Sabom suspected that the individuals had fabricated the stories to please Moody or that Moody himself had embellished the tales to help sell his book.

A MORE SCIENTIFIC APPROACH

Sabom decided to undertake his own, more scientific, study. As a cardiologist with access to the intensive care units of two hospitals, he was in an excellent position to do so. His study was to be more carefully structured than Moody's. He developed an approach and a neutral line of questioning designed to elicit such experiences without prejudicing the account. He taped interviews with patients and carefully gathered data on their medical situations, including their hospital medical records. Above all, he wished to refute the claim that people could visually witness medical resuscitation procedures from a vantage point outside their bodies. Sabom had participated in well over a hundred such resuscitations and knew that lay people would be unaware of various medical details of these procedures. If he encountered anyone who claimed to have had witnessed such procedures "out of body," he "intended to probe meticulously for details that would not ordinarily be known to nonmedical personnel." As he later wrote:

> In essence, I would pit my experience as a trained cardiologist against the professed visual recollections of lay individuals. In so doing, I was convinced that obvious inconsistencies would appear which would reduce these purported visual observations to no more than an "educated guess" on the part of the patient.[6]

Sabom began his study in two Florida hospitals. In 1978, having completed his cardiology training, he moved to Atlanta to take a position as assistant professor at Emory University School of Medicine and staff physician at the Atlanta Veterans Administration Hospital. Over a five-year period he interviewed and compiled data on 116 persons who had had a close brush with death. Of these, 71 reported one form or another of near-death experience.[7]

The elements that Moody had ascribed to the near-death experience were accurately reflected in the tales of Sabom's 71 subjects. (In 1980 psychologist Kenneth Ring published an extensive, scientifically structured study of 102 people who had had close brushes with death; it also confirmed the patterns identified by Moody.)[8] Many subjects in Sabom's sample reported having what he called "transcendental" NDEs: a sense of the ineffability of the experience, travel through the "tunnel," encounters with Christ, meetings with relatives who had died. Two had "life reviews." But also included in his sample were 32 patients who claimed to have drifted outside their bodies and observed resuscitation procedures from a vantage point above or beside the event. Sabom classed these as "autoscopic" experiences (that is, "self-perceiving"). True to his original aim, he carefully probed for details. He compared their accounts not only with his own knowledge of such procedures but also with the patients' medical records. In 26 out of the 32 cases, patients had only a general recollection of the procedure. Even so, their recollections corresponded well with accepted medical procedure. Still, in Sabom's judgment, these accounts were too vague to permit drawing any firm conclusions.[9]

PERCEPTIONS OUT OF BODY

But in six cases the recollections were extremely detailed and specific. Moreover, four additional people claimed to have witnessed their surgeries out of body.[10] (Sabom treated the surgical experiences separately, since in these cases the out-of-body experience was unaccompanied by any perception by the patient of having "died.") Sabom conducted extended interviews with the ten who had detailed recollections, either of resuscitations or surgery. The results were astonishing. In every case, the accounts jibed with standard medical procedures; moreover, where medical records were available, the records of the procedures and the accounts of patients perfectly matched. In all of these cases, patients observed details that they could not possibly have observed from their physical vantage point (to say nothing of the fact that they were for the most part unconscious, in shock, or under anesthetic while the procedures were taking place).

In one instance, a fifty-two-year-old night watchman from rural Florida gave Sabom a detailed account of his open-heart surgery, which he claimed to have observed from a vantage point above the operating table. The account matched point for point the report written up by the surgeon. Here is a short excerpt:

> They had finished draping me, the anesthesiologist had started his stuff, and all of a sudden I became aware of it . . . like I was in the room a couple of feet or so above my head, like I was another person in the room. . . . I can remember parts of the conversation that went on in there and that surprised me. . . . They had all kinds of instruments stuck in that aperture. I think they're called clamps, clamped all over the place. I was amazed that I had thought there would be blood all over the place, but there really wasn't that much blood. . . . And the heart doesn't look like I thought it did. It's big. And this is after the doctor had taken little pieces of it off. It's not shaped like I thought it would be. My heart was shaped something like the continent of Africa. Bean-shaped is another way you could describe it. Maybe mine is odd-shaped. . . . [The surface was] pinkish and yellow. I thought the yellow part was fat tissue or something. Yucky, kind of. One general area to the right or left was darker than the rest instead of it all being the same color. . . . I could draw you a picture of the saw they used to separate the ribs with.[11]

Sabom set the man's blow-by-blow account of the operation side by side with the report written by the surgeon. They matched detail for detail—as Sabom wrote, "as if he had visually witnessed the procedure."

Patient's Description	Surgeon's Description
"my head was covered and the rest of my body was draped with more than one sheet, separate sheets laid in layers."	"draped in the customary sterile fashion"
"I could draw you a picture of the saw they used."	"The sternum was sawed open in the midline"
"the thing they used to separate the ribs with. It was always there. . . . It was draped all around but you could see the metal part of it. . . . That thing they held my chest open with, that's real good steel with no rust, I mean, no discoloration. Real good, hard, shiny metal."	"a self-retaining retractor was utilized over wound towels"
"One general area to the right or left was darker than the rest instead of all being the same color."	"the ventricular aneurysm was dissected free. . . . The aneurysm was seen to be very large"

In another case, a man who encountered an autoscopic NDE in the middle of a cardiac arrest—observing the procedure, as he reported, from a point above the event, near the ceiling—described in surprising detail how the nurse prepared the defibrillator and how his body "leapt" off the bed when the defibrillator discharged:

[Subject]: Well, she reached over and got [the paddles] off the machine like this and either wiped them off or touched them together like that and everybody moved back away from it.

Patient's Description	Surgeon's Description
"He cut pieces of my heart off. He raised it and twisted it this way and that way and took quite a bit of time examining it and looking at different things."	"An incision was made over the most prominent portion of the aneurysm after the heart had been turned upside down in the pericardial wall. . . ."
"injected something into my heart. That's scary when you see that thing go right into your heart."	"Air was evacuated from the left ventricle with a needle and syringe"
"they took some stitches inside me first before they did the outside."	"the wound was closed in layers. . . . The pectoral fascia was reapproximated with interrupted sutures of 2-0 Tevdek . . . subcutaneous tissue was closed with 3-0 chronic . . . skin was closed with 4-0 nylon."[12]

First she put this one here [on chest] and then she touched me here and that's about it.

[Author]: How did she make the machine work? Did you see that?

S: There was a switch on it. Them things were there on top and there was a switch down on the right-hand side. I've never seen one of these machines before believe me. . . .

A: Did you see your body when they shocked it?

S: Yeah, it jumped about that high [gestured about one foot]. . . .

A: Had you ever seen that before happen to anyone?

S: Yeah, I seen it on TV like Medical Center or something like that. But I flopped higher than they did [on TV]. It just jars you like that on TV. It seemed like I bounced this high off the bed, you know. . . .

A: Could you see the tops of [the doctors'] heads?

S: Yeah. Dr. E is pretty thin-headed right up there [on top of head], and I've only seen him about three times. I usually see Dr. F. He's got thin hair here and the guy that was in the room with him was real bald-headed and the nurse had her hair down back like this. She had on a little white cap.[13]

Again, Sabom matched the man's account (from which the above is excerpted) with the medical records, with which it squared perfectly. He was struck by some telling details: the nurse's rubbing the paddles together (a common procedure to spread the lubricant to ensure good skin contact), the fact that everyone "stepped back" before the shock was administered. Not only did the man's account seem far more detailed than circa-1970 television portrayals of these procedures, but for obvious technical reasons, television dramas are unable to depict a key feature of the resuscitation process that the man said he witnessed—the body leaping a foot in the air as a result of the defibrillator's jolt. (It probably comes as news to most readers, as it did to me, that one would actually be flying off the bed at this moment.)

In yet another case, a retired Air Force pilot who had suffered a massive heart attack in a hospital cardiac care unit described drifting out of his body to an indeterminate point near the foot of the bed. He watched with an almost detached interest as the medical team frantically worked to revive him. He recounted the process in rich detail, even correctly describing the operation of the meter on the heart defibrillator—a detail he could not possibly have seen from where he lay incapacitated, with eyes closed, heart stopped, in bed. Here is an excerpt from Sabom's interview:

S: They had oxygen on me before, one of those little nose tubes, and they took that off and put on a face mask which covers your mouth and nose. It was a type of pressure thing. I remember, instead of the oxygen just being there, it was hissing like under pressure. Seems like someone was holding that thing most of the time.

A: Holding it over your face?

S: Right.

A: Could you describe how it looked?

S: It was sort of a soft plastic mask, light green color.

A: Was it attached to anything?

S: The hose going to the oxygen was all.

A: As far as you could tell, from where you were, would this mask have obstructed your vision if your eyes had been open?

S: Well, the way I was lying, the only way I could have seen would have been straight up, 'cause I was lying on my back.

A: Do you remember any of the other details that went on in the room?

S: I remember them pulling over the cart, the defibrillator, the thing with the paddles on it. I remember they asked for so many watt-seconds or something on the thing, and they gave me a jolt with it.

A: Did you notice any of the details of the machine itself or the cart it was sitting on?

S: I remember it had a meter on the face. I assume it read the voltage, or current, or watt-seconds, or whatever they program the thing for.

A: Did you notice how the meter looked?

S: It was square and had two needles on there, one fixed and one which moved.

A: How did it move?

S: It seemed to come up rather slowly, really. It didn't just pop up like an ammeter or a voltmeter or something registering.

A: How far up did it go?

S: The first time it went between one-third and one-half scale. And then they did it again, and this time it went up over one-half scale, and the third time it was about three-quarters.

A: What was the relationship between the moving needle and the fixed needle?

S: I think the first needle moved each time they punched the thing and somebody was messing with it. And I think they moved the fixed needle and it stayed still while the other one moved up. . . .

Note that at the time the man reported impassively observing the movement of the defibrillator needles his heart was *stopped*—hence the need for the three chargings of the machine and the three "jolts."

> **A:** Had you seen a resuscitation before?
>
> **S:** No. I never had.
>
> **A:** Had you watched it on a TV program?
>
> **S:** I don't recall ever having seen it on TV.
>
> **A:** Had you ever watched or seen this defibrillator work before?
>
> **S:** Never.[14]

The account includes many other details. But most revealing was the description of the defibrillator meter. Sabom explained:

> I was particularly fascinated by his description of a "fixed" needle and a "moving" needle on the face of the defibrillator as it was being charged with electricity. The movement of these two needles is not something he could have observed unless he had actually seen this instrument in use. These two needles are individually used (1) to preselect the amount of electricity to be delivered to the patient ("they moved the fixed needle and it stayed still") and (2) to indicate that the defibrillator is being charged to the preselected amount—"[the moving needle] seemed to come up rather slowly

really. It didn't just pop up like an ammeter or voltmeter or something registering." This charging procedure is only performed immediately prior to defibrillation, since once charged, this machine poses a serious electrical hazard unless it is correctly discharged in a very specific manner. Moreover, the meters of the type described by this man are not found on more recent defibrillator models, but were in common use in 1973, at the time of his cardiac arrest.[15]

Even assuming that the patient had some ability to perceive his surroundings, someone in the middle of a cardiac arrest, being jolted by electricity, and almost certainly unconscious, would not be at leisure to methodically observe the behavior of needles on a dial—which he was not in a physical position to see in any event.

In still another case, a woman provided a detailed and medically accurate account of her lumbar disk surgery—performed with the patient in a prone position. One of the details that she claimed to have noticed, and reacted to with some surprise, is that the chief resident in neurosurgery (whom she hadn't seen before the operation) actually performed the procedure, rather than her own attending surgeon, as she had expected. Sabom checked her medical records. Sure enough, while her chart before the operation was annotated in the hand of her attending surgeon, the actual report of the surgery was written by the chief resident, along with all subsequent markings on her chart.[16]

In another instance, a man reported leaving his body and traveling down the hall—and seeing his wife, his eldest son, and his daughter, who had arrived at the hospital on a surprise visit in the midst of the man's cardiac arrest. Sabom interviewed the wife separately. Indeed, she reported that she was startled to learn the next day from her husband that he knew of her presence; he was already in the midst of a "code 99" when she arrived. She was also further surprised that he knew precisely who had accompanied her to the hospital, since she tended to visit the hospital in the company of different family members each time she came.[17]

ALTERNATIVE EXPLANATIONS

How does one find a naturalistic explanation for such detailed observations? Susan Blackmore, a lecturer in psychology at the University of Bristol and one of the leading proponents of a purely physiological explanation of the NDE, argues that procedures "felt" by the patient or auditory cues, even under anesthesia, might be translated by the brain into an image.[18] If this were established—and there is no specific evidence for this phenomenon gathered from postsurgical patients—it might account for a certain class of observations that autoscopic experiencers report, but only a portion of them. How do we explain the laborer who saw the large dark aneurysm on his heart or saw his heart being moved about and examined by the surgeon—something that the nerves in the heart are not wired to sense, even if the anesthetic failed to cut off sensation? How do we explain a man observing his wife, daughter, and son down the hall? And then why would not most people who have gone into surgery have such recollections? In reality, Sabom found these accurate observations only among those who claimed to have had these unusual out-of-body experiences.

To test alternative hypotheses, Sabom interviewed a "control group" of twenty-five repeat cardiac patients who did not claim to have had an NDE. He probed their knowledge of resuscitation procedures. Twenty-three agreed to attempt to describe them. In sharp contrast to the NDE experiencers, the vast majority of these control group patients (twenty out of twenty-three) made serious errors in describing resuscitation. The other three offered limited, broadly accurate descriptions but, unlike the NDE experiencers, supplied few details.[19]

An even tougher case is posed by the retired Air Force pilot who observed the defibrillator meter operate. He could not have "sensed" this through his body. Implicitly acknowledging the importance of this piece of evidence, Blackmore takes up the case, noting that it was impossible to establish from medical records precisely what type of defibrillator was used:

> From these records we have no knowledge of just what kind of apparatus was used, whether the needles did move in exactly this way at the right time and so on. Yes, the man gives a plausible account and it seems unexpected given his lack of knowledge, but without access to complete details of what happened (and these can never be obtained) we cannot know just how closely it really did fit the facts at the time.[20]

Well, perhaps. But the fact that the man presented a remarkably technically correct picture of the meter operation on the type of apparatus that was commonly in use at the time of his cardiac arrest is a bit surprising. Blackmore goes on to offer an alternative explanation:

> We also have no clear idea of how much the man could have learned later, recovering in hospital or after he left. He might have been told more about the procedure afterwards. He might have become more interested in cardiac resuscitation after his own close brush with death and paid particular

attention to books, television programmes, or films about it. Without consciously intending to he might have incorporated small details from such later knowledge into his memory images, so adding to their plausibility. Five years later he could not be expected to remember where he got the information from.[21]

There are a lot of "might haves" here. But that is not the only reason why this line of analysis breaks down. First, Sabom closely questioned the man to determine if he could have gleaned the information from another source—a relevant detail, incidentally, that Blackmore fails to share with her readers. (Remember that Sabom, too, started out as a skeptic about these experiences.) According to Sabom, the man "flatly denied having ever seen this CPR procedure, including the movement of the needles on the defibrillator, at any other time." What is interesting—and lends further credibility to the account—is that this individual was unique among Sabom's cases in attaching no spiritual significance whatsoever to his experience. Sabom comments:

> The tone of the interview and of subsequent conversation I have had with this man have convinced me that he would have no reason to lie about these statements. I feel this way partly because of his consistent downplaying of the significance of his own experience throughout our conversations. While he was quite sure that he had watched his own resuscitation as if "detached, standing off to the side" and that the things he had observed were real, he nevertheless was not impressed with the experience itself.[22]

Second, as Sabom points out, the only time that the man could have observed the needles operating in such a way would have been at close quarters during an actual resuscitation. For safety reasons, the defibrillator is charged only when it is about to be used. The idea that casual knowledge gleaned about the procedure from other sources could have added up to a "false memory" of the needles moving in precisely the fashion they are supposed to move does not seem plausible. Finally, what reason do we have for discounting the man's own account of how he gained access to this highly technical information? There was no motive for lying (Sabom did not reward patients for sharing these accounts). On balance, one would have to say that Sabom's analysis of the data is less prejudicial than Blackmore's—which appears to be driven by an a priori conviction that something like this simply *couldn't* be true. (Interestingly, in her most recent book, Blackmore appears to have backed off significantly from the confident position that physiology alone can explain such phenomena. Famous to British television viewers as that country's "house skeptic," she still does not accept the existence of a nonmaterial "soul" but, by her own account, arrived at an emotional position, as she puts it, of "I don't know, I don't know, *I don't know.*" And while continuing to deny the existence of God, she has taken up Buddhist meditation.)[23]

"MOMMY AND PETER ARE WAITING"

Sabom's is by no means the only research giving evidence of this nonphysical or out-of-body perception on the part of near-death experiencers.[24] It is just the hardest to quarrel with, given his initial skepticism, the meticulous care of his methods, and the unique access he had to patients and their medical records. Certainly, Blackmore's purported refutation of this particular case does not hold up under close scrutiny.

In truth, there are many of these reports, coming from what we would have to regard as basically reliable sources. Such anecdotal evidence cannot be regarded as "scientific," but it is relevant to a reasoned evaluation of the case.

Kübler-Ross cites similar mysteries based on her work with dying children. Children who have been involved in family car accidents frequently report that loved ones are already waiting for them on the other side. She writes:

> There are a great number of car accidents in our country in which several people are injured or killed, especially on holiday weekends like Labor Day, Memorial Day, or the Fourth of July. If several people are injured and/or killed in an accident, the injured children are usually taken to the nearest hospital and, depending on the circumstance and the severity of their injury, later transferred to more specialized centers. Rarely is a child ever informed as to how many members of the family were killed at the site of the accident. . . .
>
> Shortly before children die there is often a very "clear moment," as I call it. Those who have remained in a coma since the accident or after the surgery open their eyes and seem very coherent. Those who have had great pain and discomfort are very quiet and at peace. It is in those moments that I asked them if they were willing to share what they were experiencing.
>
> "Yes, everything is all right now. Mommy and Peter are already waiting for me," one boy replied. With a content little smile, he slipped back into a coma from which he made the transition we call death.
>
> I was quite aware that his mother had died at the scene of the accident, but Peter had not died. He had been brought

to a special burn unit in another hospital, because the car had caught fire before he was extricated from the wreck. Since I was only collecting data, I accepted the boy's information and determined to look in on Peter. It was not necessary, however, because as I passed the nursing station there was a call from the other hospital to inform me that Peter had died a few minutes earlier.

In all the years that I have quietly collected data from California to Sydney, Australia; from white and black children, aboriginals, Eskimos, South Americans, and Libyan youngsters, every single child who mentioned that someone was waiting for them mentioned a person who actually preceded them in death, if only by a few moments. And yet none of these children had been informed of the recent death of the relatives by us at any time. Coincidence? By now there is no scientist or statistician who could convince me that this occurs, as some colleagues claim, as "a result of oxygen deprivation" or for other "rational and scientific" reasons.[25]

Kübler-Ross's account cannot be counted "scientific" evidence for a phenomenon. There is no full presentation of data, to say nothing of the usual controls. But unless she is simply lying—which one doubts—there is indeed no "rational and scientific" explanation for children to have access to such knowledge.

Moreover, Kübler-Ross's findings are echoed by those of other investigators, often researchers who started out as skeptics. For example, the Seattle-based physician Melvin Morse began a study of near-death experiences among children, after a little girl, "Katie," whom he resuscitated following a swimming-pool accident reported (during a routine follow-up visit) having gone to heaven in the presence of a female guide named "Elizabeth" and talked with "Jesus" and "the Heavenly

Father." Morse, too, was unprepared to encounter this phenomenon and began his research as a skeptic. But Katie's experience had several other puzzling features. For example, during her near-death experience, she recounted, she "traveled" out of body to her home, where she observed her brother moving a G.I. Joe in a jeep and her sister playing with a Barbie doll, her father sitting in the living room, and her mother cooking. "Later, when Katie mentioned this to her parents," Morse writes, "she shocked them with vivid details about the clothes they were wearing, their positions in the house, even the food her mother was cooking."[26]

The investigation of such experiences among children yields especially interesting evidence, since children work from such a small knowledge base. One teenager interviewed by Morse accurately described his resuscitation from cardiac arrest at age eleven, which he claimed to have witnessed from a vantage point above in the emergency room. The account was medically accurate in every detail. "An eleven-year-old cannot describe an emergency room resuscitation with any great accuracy," writes Morse, "no matter how much television he watches."[27]

The phenomenon of autoscopic perception forms the core of the NDE mystery. One could imagine finding a purely physiological explanation for any of the visionary elements of the experience but not for out-of-body perceptions that have been independently corroborated. Is the evidence in any sense conclusive? It remains for the reader to decide. But note that Blackmore's attempt to refute one of Sabom's more compelling cases does not hold up well under scrutiny—and there has probably been no more articulate or respected advocate of the naturalistic explanation for these phenomena than Blackmore. At the very least, late-twentieth-century medicine has stumbled on a set of phenomena that raise serious doubts about a purely physiological or materialistic model for the human consciousness or self. Assuming that one does not dismiss such reports as mere fabrications, we seem to be in the presence of at least preliminary evidence for the independent existence of a "soul."

PHYSIOLOGICAL EXPLANATIONS

Moreover, the effort to provide a purely physiological explanation for NDEs has run into another set of problems, based purely on neuroscience considerations. Researchers have been able to induce what appear to be certain fragmentary elements of an NDE-like experience—notably, feelings of ecstasy, a sense of another's "presence," and an "out-of-body-*like*" experience—through chemical or electronic stimulation. But there are theoretical problems with physiologically accounting for the near-death experience as a whole. The major difficulty lies in the contrast between the clarity and detail of the experiences, as typically reported, and the presumably debilitated condition of the brain when they occur. As the renowned British neuropsychiatrist Peter Fenwick, a Fellow of the Royal College of Psychiatrists and president of the British branch of the International Association of Near-Death Studies, writes:

> Physiology tells us that in these conditions brain processes will be distorted, and the model created by the brain will lose precision and become confused. A truly disorganised brain should not be able to produce clear psychological images. And yet what emerges from all these accounts is the startling clarity of the images seen. If the [out-of-body experience] is

indeed only a product of brain function, then we need to look for clear evidence that a disorganised brain is capable of maintaining a psychological process with the degree of clarity that is reported. At the moment this is still lacking.[28]

This is to say nothing of the evidence of autoscopic perception by people who claim to have drifted out of their bodies.

Let us look at the major alternative explanations.

Anoxia

One of the most popular hypotheses has been that the NDE results from anoxia, or oxygen starvation of the brain. (Blackmore was a proponent of this theory, in combination with the hypercarbia thesis, which is discussed below.)[29] But people who experience anoxia, either in real life (mountain climbers and fighter pilots, for example) or in laboratories, suffer distorted mental processes—deep confusion followed by a rapid descent into unconsciousness. Fenwick writes:

> As the brain becomes anoxic it ceases to function. It becomes disrupted and disorganised, so that you become gradually confused, disorientated, your perception fragments and finally you become unconscious. You do not think clearly, you don't have insights, you don't have clear, coherent visions. . . . [I]f anoxia is to be the major cause of NDEs we have to postulate a series of very unlikely events. The brain has to be able to synthesize a complex internal world and to be able to remember it, despite a lack of oxygen which is so profound that brain function is widely disrupted so that consciousness is lost.[30]

Add to this the fact that there is no systematic evidence to show that near-death experiences occur during periods of anoxia.[31] Sabom found one case (discussed following) of a patient whose blood gases were measured during an out-of-body experience: His oxygen level was above normal.

Interestingly, Fenwick collected one NDE account by a former RAF pilot who had separately experienced anoxia during his flying days. He described a sharp contrast between the anoxic state and the NDE:

> I found myself "floating" along in a dark tunnel, peacefully and calmly but wide awake and aware. I know that the tunnel experience has been attributed to the brain being deprived of oxygen, but as an ex-pilot who has experienced lack of oxygen at altitude I can state that for me there was no similarity. On the contrary the whole [NDE] experience from beginning to end was crystal clear and it has remained so for the past fifteen years.[32]

Frequently in near-death cases there is a disconnect between the condition of the brain and the quality of the recollection. In one case a woman recounted to Fenwick a near-death experience that she had when she was assaulted by her husband, who, without warning, slammed a hammer into her skull from behind. People who suffer such a severe head injury, Fenwick notes, have no memory of the event and suffer memory disruption for significant periods of time. Instead, the woman recounted a vivid near-death experience during her period of unconsciousness, involving lengthy conversations with spirit beings on the question of the advisability of her "returning" to her earthly life; she claimed on awakening that she knew precisely what had happened to her—a recollection impossible to explain in neurophysiological terms.[33]

Hallucination

One of the earliest hypotheses offered for the NDE was that it was a hallucination (possibly drug-induced) or a dream.[34] Not only do many people encounter NDEs with no drug involvement, but also, as a number of researchers have argued, the experience does not have the normal characteristics of a hallucination. First, the otherwise normal people who have near-death experiences do not interpret them as hallucinations, but as very "real" experiences—"as real as you and me sitting here talking" is a common characterization. Normally those who experience hallucinations are aware afterwards that they have been hallucinating. Sabom had two patients who had each experienced drug-induced hallucinations and a near-death experience on separate occasions. Both perceived sharp distinctions between the hallucinatory state and the NDE. Second, hallucinations normally involve serious distortions of reality. But the NDE is normally ordered. While imagery may vary, the experience is remembered as highly coherent. Moreover, there are common patterns to the experience, across individuals and across cultures,[35] whereas hallucinations tend to be more idiosyncratic. Third, hallucinations are characteristically accompanied by anxiety and disturbance; the vast majority of those who report having had NDEs describe a feeling of peace and calm once they have separated from their bodies. Fourth, a number of studies have shown that NDEs normally have a life-transforming effect on the beliefs, attitudes, and behaviors of those who experience them. Diminished fear of death is among the most universal aftereffects. A heightened sense of spirituality and purpose—often reflected in major lifestyle changes—is also common.[36]

Mere hallucinations do not normally have this kind of carry-over into individuals' lives.

Finally, certain peculiarities of the experience distinguish it sharply from dream states, as Fenwick notes. Sleep studies show that time in dreams correlates closely with ordinary waking time. NDEs are quite different from this. Experiencers typically report the realm beyond death to be without time in the ordinary sense of that term. The narratives that they bring back occasionally recount events that in normal, earthly time would unfold over many hours or even days, though typically the person is "gone"—dead, unconscious, whatever—for no more than a matter of minutes.[37]

Birth Tunnel Memory

The late Carl Sagan, an outspoken agnostic, theorized that the tunnel perceived by many near-death experiencers was a memory of birth, a theory that gained adherents until it was pointed out that the eyesight of babies is too poor to perceive the birth canal.[38]

Endorphins

Given the lack of pain that near-death experiencers report during the period out of body, other researchers have theorized that the NDE could be the product of a massive release of endorphins—morphine-like natural painkillers. However, as Fenwick explains, neither artificial nor natural opiates have been shown to induce the NDE state. Injecting patients with morphine will not bring on an NDE or even feelings of ecstasy. Patients who suffer grand mal seizures have unusually high endorphin levels following the episode. But rather than feeling ecstatic, they feel drained and exhausted.[39] Moreover, as Sabom already pointed out in his study in the early 1980s, it requires a matter of hours for the body to remove the excess endorphins. That should provide an extended period of relief from pain. But, characteristically, near-death experiencers who have the experience during a resuscitation report a recurrence of pain immediately after "returning" to their bodies after the few-minutes-long NDE.

Hypercarbia

Another hypothesis has attributed the experience to elevated levels of carbon dioxide in the brain. In the 1950s, the American psychiatrist L. J. Meduna experimented with mixtures of oxygen and carbon dioxide administered to patients as psychiatric therapy. Patients recorded a variety of sensory imagery in response to the treatments, some of which strongly resembled the imagery of the NDE: "I felt as though I was looking down at myself, as though I was way out here in space. . . . I felt sort of separated," said one. Another recorded: "It was a wonderful feeling. It was marvelous. I felt very light and I didn't know where I was. . . . And then I thought that something was happening to me. This wasn't night. I wasn't dreaming. . . . And then I felt a wonderful feeling as if I was out in space." Still another said:

> I felt myself being separated; my soul drawing apart from the physical being, was drawn upward seemingly to leave the earth and to go upward where it reached a greater Spirit with

Whom there was a communion, producing a remarkable, new relaxation and deep security. Through this communion I seemed to receive assurance that the little problems or whatever was bothering the human being that was huddled down on Earth, would work out all right and that I had no need to worry.[40]

This is strikingly similar to an NDE. Not all patients had these experiences: Others saw brightly colored patterns, fantasized objects, experienced a compulsion to solve mathematical puzzles, or saw horrifying objects and awoke in terror.

Given the NDE-like experience of some patients, would hypercarbia be a good candidate for explaining the NDE? It seems unlikely, since hospitals would be remiss if they permitted elevated blood carbon dioxide levels in, for example, heart attack patients. Interestingly, Sabom had one patient who reported witnessing, out of body, an "injection" into his groin area during a resuscitation, which turned out to be a measurement of blood gases taken by the medical team using a syringe. Sabom was able to track down the medical report with the blood gas readings (which, as the patient correctly reported, was taken from the femoral artery in the groin). The patient readings showed *excess* oxygen (the normal consequence of administering oxygen to heart attack victims) and *below-normal* carbon dioxide. So there is at least one fully documented counterexample to the hypercarbia theory. But what explains the NDE-like experiences of some of Meduna's patients? It turns out that patients' reactions to the treatment were often quite violent. Pupils became rigid, eyes rolled upward, and patients suffered violent seizures that continued after the mask was removed, followed by a prolonged stupor.

So pronounced were these symptoms that Sabom raises the possibility that Meduna's treatments may have actually induced a physical near-death crisis in some of his subjects, triggering the onset of an NDE. At any event, it is unlikely, to put it mildly, that such research would be repeated in the present climate of medical liability.

Temporal Lobe Involvement

Fenwick suggests a possible role for the right temporal lobe of the brain in the NDE. Many features of the near-death experience would correlate with what is known about the right temporal lobe: It is thought to be the seat of emotion, to provide the sense of existential certainty of experience. Individuals who sustain damage to the right temporal lobe can have a distorted sense of time.[41] A researcher at Canada's Laurentian University, Michael Persinger, stimulated the right temporal lobe of 200 volunteers electromagnetically. About a quarter reported experiencing an "out-of-body-like" experience and the sense of another "presence" near them. (Most just felt dizziness and tingling.)[42] (Persinger's laboratory is committed to proving that *all* religious experience is reducible to intrusions of right temporal lobe consciousness on the left temporal lobe, but for now this is no more than a theory.)[43] But such transient perceptions hardly add up to a persuasive model for the entire NDE, which, as Fenwick notes, can include language, body image, narrative line, even smells—factors that are known to involve other parts of the brain.[44]

* * *

What we can say with certainty is this: At present no accepted physiological theory can explain the near-death experience, and some lines of inquiry that once looked very promising—such as hallucination and anoxia—look much less promising today. This is not to foreclose the possibility that science may explain more of the phenomenon as time passes. Some researchers, like Morse, believe that even if the NDE is transcendental in character, there is still likely to be a physiological substratum, at least for the early stages of the experience.[45] But what we have at present is just hypothesis and speculation—side by side with the still-unexplained evidence, from Sabom and others, of seemingly accurate out-of-body perceptions on the part of near-death experiencers.

RELIGIOUS DIMENSIONS

Physicians and scientists were not the only ones to look critically on the near-death experience when it emerged into the public eye. Some religious authorities were also quite uncomfortable with the concept. Conservative Christians, in particular, were unhappy that the NDE seemed at odds with certain interpretations of Christian doctrine. *Christianity Today*, the usually quite sensible flagship journal of evangelical Christians, editorialized negatively on the near-death experience a year after Moody's book appeared:

> Before Christians run to jump on the bandwagon or add these data to their apologetic arsenal, they should be aware that no essential difference is reported between the OBEs [out-of-body experiences] of believers and unbelievers! All testify to a distinctively positive experience—a feeling of perfect peace, floating outside the body, restoration to whole-

ness (in the case of those who have lost limbs), hearing beautiful music, and the like. Christians testify to seeing Christ while Hindus say they come face to face with Krishna. Cultists tend to have their worldview validated, and some nominal Christians adopt heterodox opinions. A Scottish Presbyterian, for example, testified: "I know beyond a doubt that the Christ I saw will accept everyone, good or bad."[46]

A Lutheran pastor writing in *The Christian Century* complained, "If life after death could be empirically verified, then there would seem little need for faith."[47]

In truth, the picture of near-death experiences presented by early research was a bit rosy and one-sided. Not until the 1990s was it gradually realized that a small but significant number of people have negative or "hellish" near-death experiences. Many near-death researchers fought bitterly against this recognition.[48] One reason that the hellish experiences may have taken longer to surface is that people who had had such experiences were understandably much more reluctant to share them with researchers than were the individuals who had had wholly pleasant ones. Another reason for the paucity of such reports is offered by Maurice Rawlings—a cardiologist who converted from indifferent religious views to fervent Christian evangelism after encountering a patient who claimed to have experienced "hell." Rawlings found that hellish experiences were more likely than pleasant ones to be *forgotten*.[49] (Notably, however, anecdotal reports suggest that, like the pleasant NDEs, the hellish experiences that are remembered tend to have morally transforming effects on the lives of those who have them.)[50]

At any rate, that there is a reckoning for good and evil in the afterlife has been a major theme of near-death accounts from the beginning. Even George Ritchie, whose account of his elaborate near-death experience in 1943 inspired Moody's original interest, witnessed regions in the afterworld that were unmistakably hellish in nature (though one of them seemed to be "physically" located on earth).[51] It is true that near-death experiencers who report a life review generally say that it is they, rather than Christ or some authority figure, who perform the judgment, but this is no more than a detail. The life is reviewed with the assistance of Christ or "the Light," which provides the framework for judgment. One should not forget that Bible texts are notoriously laconic on the question of the nature of the realm beyond this life. Even Paul, who recorded a mystical vision in which he was "caught up to the third heaven" (2 Corinthians 12:2), stresses that "We see in a mirror dimly" (1 Corinthians 13:12) when it comes to the world beyond.

In reality, the cumulative theology of the near-death experience—if it can be called that—tends to add to its plausibility. For it tracks very closely with that of the Bible—and with a core moral vision in many respects common to all major religions—while failing to confirm some of the detailed doctrines, and certainly the prejudices, of particular sects. Moreover, the fact that most experiencers report surprise at the manner in which their experiences unfolded and at what they learned also adds a dimension of credibility: The experiencer's conventional expectations about the afterlife are generally not confirmed, even though the moral framework conveyed by the experience is fully compatible with, for example, the New Testament teachings of Jesus. The recurring theme that emerges from those who have had such experiences is that one is responsible for every thought, word, and deed of one's life and that all are to be judged in light of the universal law of love. It is worth looking at one of the more extended "life reviews" reported to Moody:

When the light appeared, the first thing he said to me was "What do you have to show me that you've done with your life?" or something to this effect. And that's when these flashbacks started. I thought, "Gee, what is going on?" because, all of a sudden, I was back in my early childhood. And from then on, it was like I was walking from the time of my very early life, right up to the present.

It was really strange where it started, too, when I was a little girl, playing down by the creek in our neighborhood, and there were other scenes from about that time—experiences I had had with my sister, and things about neighborhood people, and actual places I had been. And then I was in kindergarten, and I remembered the time when I had this one toy I really liked, and I broke it and cried for a long time. . . . I remembered when I was in Girl Scouts and went camping, and remembered many things about all the years of grammar school. . . .

The things that flashed back came in the order of my life, and they were so vivid. The scenes were just like if you walked outside and saw them, completely three-dimensional, and in color. And they moved. For instance, when I saw myself breaking the toy, I could see all the movements. It wasn't like I was watching it all from my perspective at the time. It was like the little girl was somebody else, in a movie. . . .

Now, I didn't actually see the light as I was going through the flashbacks. He disappeared as soon as he asked me what I had done, and the flashbacks started, and yet I knew that he was there with me the whole time, that carried me back through the flashbacks, because I felt his presence, and because he made comments here and there. He was trying to show me something in each one of these flashbacks. . . .

All through this, he kept stressing the importance of love. The places where he showed it best involved my sister; I have always been very close to her. He showed me some instances where I had been selfish to my sister. . . .

He seemed very interested in things concerning knowledge, too. He kept on pointing out things that had to do with learning, and he did say that I was going to continue learning. . . .[52]

Another man reported the regret and shame that has been characteristically experienced by many who have undergone the life review:

I first was out of my body, above the building, and I could see my body just lying there. Then I became aware of the light—just light—being all around me. Then it seemed there was a display all around me, and everything just went by for review, you might say. I was really very, very ashamed of a lot of the things that I experienced because it seemed that I had a different knowledge, that the light was showing me what was wrong, what I did wrong. And it was very real.

It seemed like this flashback, or memory, or whatever was directed primarily at ascertaining the extent of my life. It was like there was a judgment being made and then, all of a sudden, the light became dimmer, and there was a conversation, not in words, but in thoughts. When I would see something, when I would experience a past event, it was like I was seeing through eyes with (I guess you would say) omnipotent knowledge, guiding me, and helping me to see.

That's the part that has stuck with me, because it showed me not only what I had done but *even how what I had done had affected other people.* And it wasn't like I was looking at a movie projector because I could *feel* these things; there was feeling, and particularly since I was with this knowledge . . . I found out that not even your thoughts are lost. . . . Every thought was there. . . . Your thoughts are not lost. . . .[53]

The figure of Christ prominently recurs in the more elaborate examples of these visions, sometimes seen as a person, sometimes as the identity that the experiencer ascribes to the "Being of Light." Some Christians, perhaps especially certain fundamentalist believers, place great emphasis on the notion of Christ as "judge" of the "living" and the "dead." Near-death experiencers who claim to encounter Christ are struck instead by an overwhelming sense of unconditional love and compassion emanating from Him. He is not *judgmental*. But there is also a very firm, uncompromising law of right and wrong, based on a central ethic of love, which he conveys implicitly, frequently causing shame or embarrassment in the experiencer as he or she reviews the actions of a lifetime.[54] But this is precisely the impression that one forms of the Jesus of the New Testament ("Let he who is without sin cast the first stone")—though not necessarily the one always emphasized on Sunday in church. George Ritchie described the Christ he encountered in his extended 1943 near-death experience as a "Man made out of light," mixing primeval antiquity with vast sophistication. "This Person was power itself, older than time and yet more modern than anyone I had ever met," he wrote. According to Ritchie, the figure indicated to him during his life review that the purpose of life is to love other human beings. When Ritchie thought indignantly, "Someone should have told me," the response of Christ is simple and straightforward: *"I did tell you. . . . I told you by the life I lived. I told you by the death I died."*[55]

The fact that Hindus encounter Hindu religious figures rather than the figure of Christ should hardly be surprising even to Christians. "Heaven" would be a rough place indeed if an individual who was born and reared in the Hindu religion would be greeted upon the moment of death by Christian religious figures announcing that he or she had adhered through earthly life to the wrong religion! Indeed, one of the lessons that near-death experiencers recurrently report is that of the need for religious tolerance.[56] Kübler-Ross theorizes that individuals are greeted by the figure that best suits their needs—be it a deceased relative (the most common case, studies show, among American experiencers), Jesus, or—say, for devotional Catholics—Mary.[57]

One cannot attach too much significance to any single near-death report—each, after all, is filtered through the subjectivity of an individual. But cumulatively they convey a reassuring sense that, so to speak, there is intelligent life in the universe. The methods and perspectives of the otherworld, as they are conveyed in these accounts, are neither narrow nor bureaucratic. (An exception is some Hindu experiences, which, while following the outlines of the Western ones, occasionally give the experience a more bureaucratic flavor.)[58] They seem enlightened. They add insight to Gospel passages and other sacred literature rather than detracting from them. The ethical messages that experiencers claim to receive are consonant with the highest and best thinking about morality that we know.

The lesson that love should prove to be the central value that we are supposed to learn and practice in earthly life should come as no surprise to anyone who has read the

Bible—though it is not necessarily the theme emphasized by churches across the ages (recently one senses a change for the better here).

A COMMON EXPERIENCE

When Moody's book appeared, near-death experiences were thought to be a bit outlandish. But subsequent research has shown them to be remarkably common. Findings by Sabom and others have indicated that roughly one-third of people who have close brushes with death can be expected to have an NDE in some form—ranging from an experience of being out of the body on up to an experience of the full "transcendental" variety.[59] In a 1980–1981 Gallup poll, as many as 15 percent of respondents reported having a "close call" with death that involved "an unusual experience at that time" (though it is difficult to determine from the poll how many had an experience that would fit various researchers' definitions of an NDE).[60] Doubtless the prevalence of these experiences may have something to do with the development of modern resuscitation techniques: Modern medicine has become more and more adept at bringing people "back from the dead." But there is evidence for the existence of such experiences throughout history. Plato's *Republic* tells the story of a near-death experience. Otherworldly journeys are recounted in both the Egyptian Book of the Dead and the Tibetan Book of the Dead.[61] Somewhat coincidentally, as I learned when I began reading about these phenomena, my wife Gabriele's paternal grandfather—who died at a ripe old age as the mayor of a tiny hamlet in Germany—apparently had such an experience when he was on the verge of passing. He seemingly "died," only to return and report to his daughter, who was caring for him, that he had been to the other side, that it was beautiful, and he had seen "Lenchen," his wife. Having reassured his grieving daughter, he passed over. The family, conventional German Catholics, did not know quite what to make of the story—indeed, there seems to be a certain uncomfortable fit and simultaneous lack of fit between stories of these experiences and orthodox religious teachings. But there it was. In fact, research shows that such apparition experiences at the point of death are extraordinarily common in cultures across the globe.[62]

Each individual will have to make his or her own judgment regarding the evidence. But in a quarter century, near-death research has produced an enormous body of data that no one honestly interested in rationally evaluating the likelihood of the existence of God can afford to ignore. It is difficult to analyze this evidence in depth and to come away with any other impression but that science has indeed stumbled on data of the soul. Certainly that was my experience in studying these accounts. It has also been the experience of the majority of near-death researchers themselves, many of whom initially approached the phenomenon, like Michael Sabom, in a skeptical spirit.

As Moody observed in a 1995 interview:

When I first heard about this, I assumed it was something like that, shock to the brain and so forth. I know many physicians, literally from all over the world, who have investigated this phenomenon, and they all started with that assumption. All of us, in talking with the people who have had these experiences, have come around very much in our views.

The classic definition of a hallucination, of course, is that it's an apparent sensory experience without a corresponding external event. That is, a person sees or hears something when there is not really anything there. But with these near death experiences, we have many cases where the patients, while they are out of their bodies, are able to witness something going on at a distance, even in another part of the hospital, which later turns out by independent verification to have been exactly as the patient said. So this is very difficult to put together with a simple physiological or biochemical explanation. . . .

I think that no final answer, though, can be settled on to the question you asked, because ultimately in this frontier area of the human mind, there aren't any experts there that can give us the answer. There is no conventionally established way yet to determine the answer. Everybody is going to have to look at this and make up his own mind in his own way. All I can do is speak for myself and my many colleagues in medicine who have looked into this, and we're all convinced that the patients do get a glimpse of the beyond.[63]

I suppose it is possible that some alternative explanation could be found for people to perceive things out of body that they could not have physically seen—how I don't know. I suppose it could be merely accidental that people who claim to have died and return come back with elaborate narratives and messages about ethics and life that are by and large more coherent than what one often hears in church on Sunday—even while being perfectly in line with those values. All this, one could argue, is merely the result of some accident of evolution that structured the brain to respond in a certain way to the circumstance of death. Could it be accidental? I suppose. But it would be a very strange accident indeed.

five

Reason and Spirit

S uch is the great surprise as the twentieth century turns
into the twenty-first: The very logic of human inquiry is
compelling a rediscovery of the realm of spirit, of God
and the soul. This process has both a positive and a negative
thrust. In the first place, we see the mounting evidence for the
existence of a spiritual dimension of reality. Along with this
new evidence has come a growing recognition of the severe
limitations of science and reason as tools for understanding
the ultimate truths. This recognition has been central to the
experience of twentieth-century philosophy, politics, and
science itself. A generation and more ago, secular thinkers
were filled with faith in reason and convinced that the scientific
worldview was destined to replace the religious one. Modern
thinkers predicted the "disenchantment of the world"[1]—the
disappearance of God from the human horizon. What our
century has experienced instead is a disenchantment with
reason, the collapse of the Enlightenment's secular and rational
faith. Perhaps not entirely coincidentally, God is reemerging

in Western intellectual life at the very moment when reason appears to have hit the end of the road.

We indeed find ourselves in a strange cultural moment, suspended between the twilight of the old paradigm and the birth of a new one. Nowhere is this paradoxical state of affairs more apparent than in the small but academically influential world of postmodern philosophy.

POSTMODERNISM AND POSTSECULARISM

At the core of contemporary philosophy is a strange contradiction. Contemporary philosophers have inherited the legacy of the modern "death of God" thinkers. Following Nietzsche and Heidegger, they argue that reason can discover no universal values, that rational analysis shows all moral views to be radically contingent, that all our highest impulses and moral yearnings are nothing more than the products of biology and accidental historical circumstances, that reason itself in the universal sense of that term does not exist. Yet postmodern philosophers find themselves repelled by the moral vision that originally accompanied the modern "death of God" insight. Nietzsche, declaring God "dead" and dubbing himself the "Antichrist," openly preached the nobility of barbarism and cruelty.[2] His radically relativistic—and indeed deeply nasty—philosophy helped prepare the soil of German culture for the rise of the Nazi regime.[3] Nietzsche's great philosophical successor, Martin Heidegger, actually became an enthusiastic Nazi, implementing the Nazi agenda at the University of Freiburg, where he was rector in 1933–34, and refusing to condemn National Socialism categorically even after the war.[4]

Contemporary philosophers are understandably appalled by this, and so contemporary philosophy has become an attempt to square the circle. It tries to set forward a humane moral vision while strenuously arguing, in the manner of Nietzsche and Heidegger, that such a moral vision has absolutely no rational or other foundation. Richard Rorty, the leading American postmodern philosopher, is a case in point. While he condemns Auschwitz, he argues that there is no rational or other basis to do so. Moreover, he claims we all would be better off if, like him, we recognized no absolutes. As he writes in *Contingency, Irony, and Solidarity:*

> At times like that of Auschwitz, when history is in upheaval and traditional institutions and patterns of behavior are collapsing, we want something [i.e., universal values] which stands beyond history and institutions. . . . I have been urging in this book that we try not to want something which stands beyond history and institutions. The fundamental premise of the book is that a belief can still regulate action, can still be thought worth dying for, among people who are quite aware that this belief is caused by nothing deeper than contingent historical circumstances.[5]

Despite this relativistic perspective, Rorty spends much of his book trying to set forward a humane moral vision, based on Judith Shklar's definition of "liberals" as people who "think that cruelty is the worst thing we do."[6] His purpose is to overcome Nietzsche's "insinuation that the end of religion and metaphysics should mean the end of our attempts not to be cruel."[7] He argues that we should "try to extend our sense of 'we' to people whom we have previously thought of as 'they.'" He calls for human beings to deepen their empathy and compassion and extend their capacities to overlook tribal, cultural, religious, and other differences, to move toward a more and more inclusive sense of "we"—a value he calls "solidarity":

> The view I am offering says that there is such a thing as moral progress, and that this progress is indeed in the direction of greater human solidarity. But that solidarity is not thought of as a recognition of a core self, the human essence, in all human beings. Rather, it is thought of as the ability to see more and more traditional differences (of tribe, religion, race, customs, and the like) as unimportant when compared with similarities with respect to pain and humiliation—the ability to think of people wildly different from ourselves as included in the range of "us."[8]

There is of course nothing wrong with this vision—apart from the issue of whether we have a "core self" (to which I will return in a moment). On the contrary, it is admirable. What is peculiar is the claim that he can find no foundation for it. He ascribes it, almost as an afterthought, to liberal "self-doubt."[9] But what could liberal "self-doubt" be if not a euphemism for "conscience"?

Yet, surely, the source and appeal of Rorty's moral vision are not so mysterious. Isn't there a familiar ring to the values that Rorty places at the center of his philosophy? Rorty actually mentions the source of these values in passing but dismisses it out of hand: Christianity. As it happens, the first text in human history to set forth a code of "solidarity"—of overcoming tribalistic differences and sympathizing with others' pain—in terms resembling those of Rorty was the New Testament. Might there not be some causal relationship here that is being overlooked?

It is instructive that the best that modern philosophy has been able to produce after hundreds of years of attempting to replace the idea of God with a comprehensive alternative based on "reason" turns out to be a diluted and less than completely coherent version of the New Testament moral vision. Certainly, this marks a major improvement over Nietzsche's vicious "master morality" or Heidegger's praise of the "inner truth and greatness" of Nazism,[10] and for that we should be grateful. It also suggests philosophy's discovery, by trial and error, sometimes big error, that the logic of moral life is indeed close to that set forth in the Gospels. But the postmodern philosopher has become a strange sort of middleman: He borrows the New Testament vision, benefits from its potent appeal, and then presents it to us claiming, incongruously, to have arrived at these moral insights on the basis of the modern discovery that there are "no values."

Yet postmodern philosophy offers a weakened and corrupted form of the New Testament outlook. Rorty's moral vision includes a large escape clause. While absolute in "public" life, it has no "*automatic* priority" in "private" life:

> Another central claim of this book, which will seem equally indecent to those who find the purity of morality attractive, is that our responsibilities to others constitute *only* the public side of our lives, a side which competes with our private affections and our private attempts at self-creation, which has no *automatic* priority over such private motives. . . . Moral obligation is, in this view, to be thrown in with a lot of other considerations, rather than automatically trump them.[11]

This is to say, presumably, that in one's private affairs, the value of "solidarity," of avoiding "cruelty" to others, may take a back seat to some other passion or priority. Rorty's analysis of Vladimir Nabokov's novel *Lolita* perhaps gives a hint of what such a private passion might be. The dilemma of the novel is that Humbert Humbert's pedophiliac passion for the underage Lolita results in cruelty to her (and this is supposed to be a profound moral lesson?).[12] Note that the New Testament makes the opposite claim: All public goodness is based on private goodness. Indeed, Jesus' most radical assertion is that we are what we think in our inmost private thoughts: A married man who desires another woman has *already* committed adultery (Matthew 5:27–28). The human evils we see in the world originate in the evil thoughts of human beings: "But the things that proceed out of the mouth come from the heart, and those defile the man. For out of the heart come evil thoughts, murder, adulteries, fornications, thefts, false witnesses, slanders" (Matthew 15:18–19).[13]

Not only is the postmodern moral vision incoherent; it is the purest hypocrisy. Such hypocrisy is not new in the history of philosophy. The world's first moral philosopher, Socrates, similarly tried to distinguish between a private realm, where there were "no values," and the morality he put forward for public consumption—as Aristophanes makes clear in his satire of Socrates in *The Clouds*. Hence Socrates' continual talk about the need for "noble lies" and so forth. Such private-public distinctions always prove unsustainable. Socrates' private irreverence and atheism were an open secret in the Athens of his day, as Aristophanes' plays demonstrate. Moreover, certain students whom Socrates initiated into the "secrets" of his amoral vision became famous for exporting this moral outlook to public life. His favorite pupil, the brilliant and unprincipled Alcibiades, was generally regarded as the most impious, self-interested, and least trustworthy politician of his day. More troublingly, Critias, another Socratic protégé, led the coup of the Thirty Tyrants, a conspiracy of oligarchs who overthrew the Athenian democracy and, in a reign of terror, executed hundreds of their fellow citizens. This was almost certainly the main reason why Socrates was ultimately put on trial for teaching immorality, "corrupting the young."[14]

THE DEACTUALIZED SELF

There is a close connection between the denial of private morality and Rorty's major teaching, which is that there is no "core self":

> The crucial move in this reinterpretation is to think of the moral self, the embodiment of rational, not as one of Rawls's original choosers, somebody who can distinguish her *self* from her talents and interests and views about the good, but as a network of beliefs, desires, and emotions with nothing behind it—no substrate behind the attributes. For purposes of moral and political deliberation and conversation, a person just *is* that network, as for purposes of ballistics she is a point-mass, or for purposes of chemistry a linkage of molecules.[15]

We have landed a long way from our planned destination in the modern quest for certainty via reason. Descartes' original foundation of all certainty, *Cogito ergo sum*, "I think, therefore I am," has now turned into its opposite: *Cogito ergo non sum*. As the proverbial Valley Girl might put it, "I think, therefore I am. Not!" Having devoured "God" and "values," reason now turns on her master, the philosopher, destroying his confidence that he can claim to have, or rather be, a "self."

Yet, peculiarly, atheistic postmodern philosophy appears to be acting out the very process that Martin Buber predicts when the human being turns his back on the "I-You" encounter with God and submerses himself in the world of materialism, rationalism, and mere "using" of things and people—the world of "I-It." The result is what Buber calls the "deactualized self":[16]

> The capricious man does not believe and encounter. He does not know association; he only knows the feverish world out there and his feverish desire to use it. . . . When he says You, he means: You, my ability to use! . . . In truth he has no destiny but is merely determined by things and drives, feels autocratic, and is capricious. He has no great will and tries to pass off caprice in its place. . . . But the unbelieving marrow of the capricious man cannot perceive anything but unbelief and caprice, positing ends and devising means. His world is devoid of sacrifice and grace, encounter and present, but shot through with ends and means: it could not be different and its name is doom. For all his autocratic bearing, he is inextricably entangled in unreality; and he becomes aware of this whenever he recollects his own condition. Therefore he takes pains to use the best part of his mind to prevent or at least obscure such recollection.[17]

Reason, freed from divine guidance, originally promised humanity freedom; but its culmination in the moral realm is postmodernism, and the spirit of postmodern thought is nothing if not the spirit of "caprice"—private projects, "play," efforts at "self-creation," erotic and aesthetic obsessions, of which Humbert Humbert's pedophiliac obsession for Lolita is an all-too-appropriate caricature. My contention is that Rorty's insight and Buber's are, peculiarly, not that far apart;

but Rorty merely presents only the negative side of it, expressing the mood of the Western mind trapped, at the "end of history," in the web of deactualization. To put the proposition as a philosopher might: Postmodernism is the self-consciousness of the deactualized self.

What Rorty values in his philosophy is precisely the opposite of what the reader is likely to value, at least in his or her heart. Everything that is appealing in Rorty's writing can be traced back to the New Testament, the notion of sympathizing with others' pain and humiliation and overcoming barriers of culture, ethnicity, race, of developing a more inclusive "we." Everything that comes from modern death-of-God philosophy—the claim that there are no values, no absolute private moral obligations—is repugnant, as Humbert Humbert is repugnant. The superficial appeal of Rorty's philosophy rests on an artful confusion of the two.

There is nothing stable about the postmodern vision as a resting place for human consciousness. The mind may insist on these nihilistic propositions, but in the long run the heart will not tolerate them. That is why Rorty can be seen reaching for a moral vision—the pale and confused reflection of New Testament *agape*, or love, that he calls "solidarity." There is already here a glimpse of the "I-You," of the "*ich-Du*," but only a glimpse. Western philosophy is like the prodigal son of Jesus' parable, at the end of his long quest for freedom. So untenable are his circumstances that even pride must eventually surrender. And pride is precisely what he must surrender before he can return to the Father. But will not the call of the Father eventually prevail? Buber writes that in ages like the modern era, where the world of "I-It" blots out the world of "I-You," "the person in the human being and in humanity comes to lead a subterranean, hidden, as it were, invalid existence—*until it is summoned.*"[18] That is why I would contend: Postmodernism is postsecularism waiting to be born.

The paradoxical position of the postmodern philosopher vis-à-vis moral questions is analogous to that of the postmodern scientist, who today can offer no explanation for the most fundamental things. Recall the astronomer Fred Hoyle's discussion of the paradoxes of modern scientific cosmology and biology:

> All that we see in the universe of observation and fact, as opposed to the mental state of scenario and supposition, remains unexplained. . . . Even in its supposedly first second the universe itself is acausal. . . . The higher qualities of Man are acausal, like the Universe itself. . . . While abilities . . . like running would have been important to the survival of primitive man, the higher qualities [such as higher mathematical and musical ability] had no survival value at all. . . . The mystery is that we have been endowed with the relevant genes in advance of them being useful.[19]

But is it not a curious coincidence that everywhere postmodern science and postmodern philosophy posit no cause, no explanation, no foundation, no ground, no reason, is precisely where the religious mind finds God? It is almost as if Western thought has been playing an elaborate intellectual game with a single overarching rule: The ultimate reality to which all the evidence points must be denied. The distinctive feature of the present era is that this game has become all too transparent.

TRIBALISM AND RELIGION

In truth, this ultimate reality has sometimes been obscured by religion itself. The prestige enjoyed by reason in the modern era came from two sources. First, and most important, of course, was the prowess of technology. Every new invention and improvement confirmed the truth of science and the power of scientific rationality. But a second source of interest in reason was the purblind intolerance and tribalism of traditional religion. Modern political and social science took shape largely in reaction to Europe's bloody religious struggles. Thomas Hobbes wrote *Leviathan*, the first great tract in social and political science, in direct response to England's religiously inspired civil war. Amid such violent religious frenzy, atheism indeed might have seemed the soul of virtue.

There is more than a grain of truth in G. K. Chesterton's observation that Christianity has not been "tried and found wanting" but "found difficult and never tried." The first text in history to speak of expanding the "we" to include those formerly regarded as "they" and to identify sympathizing with the pain of others as among the highest values was the New Testament. But the effort to embody such an insight in a human institution was, predictably, less successful in many instances than one might hope. Modern organizational theorists have noticed how bureaucracies tend to replace the goal for which they were originally established with the goal of advancing their own survival and interests. This is no less true of churches than of other human institutions. Through much of human history, even modern history, churches have been tribalistic.

The emphasis on overcoming religious tribalism, and human tribalism generally, actually forms a core message of the New Testament, one of the major emphases of the text, repeated again and again under a variety of guises. It is part of the meaning of the crucifixion itself. Christian history might have been very different if Christians had only remembered that the human motivation for killing the man they regarded as their savior and as God incarnate was religious persecution (and the cynicism of secular authorities). Those who burned witches and heretics in later centuries were repeating exactly the "sin" that killed Jesus. The fate of Jesus contradicted the Jewish cultural expectation at the time about the Messiah—though not the prophecies of Isaiah, who foresaw a man "despised and forsaken of men, a man of sorrows and acquainted with grief . . . pierced through for our transgressions . . . crushed for our iniquities" (Isaiah 53:3–5). The Jews of the Roman era expected a political and military leader in the mold of Moses or Joshua, who would liberate them from the Roman oppressor. One of the major meanings of the crucifixion appears to have been to teach human beings the importance of separating true spirituality from tribalism, communal hatred, and war making. The God of the early books of the Hebrew Bible continually instructs the leader of the Hebrews or "the Lord's anointed" to attack villages and slaughter all the inhabitants. There is clearly a confusion taking place at this much earlier stage in human history, where the experience of God is more completely submerged in the imperatives of a culture and its will to survive. Part of what is "modern" about the New Testament is the sharp separation drawn between culture and God.

The message of tolerance, of the irrelevance of cultural, ethnic, and even religious divisions, pervades the New Testament texts. When Jesus is asked to define the concept of loving one's neighbor, he tells the story of the good Samaritan, who helps a man who has been beaten by the roadside, after a priest and a Levite pass him by (Luke 29: 25–37). The priest and the Levite belonged culturally to the "holiest" rank in first-century Jewish society. Samaritans were viewed as an "unclean" race, literally *Untermenschen*.[20] (Jews and Samaritans had feelings for each other resembling those of today's Serbs and Croats, only more intense.) In the gospel of John, Jesus converses with and accepts a drink from a Samaritan woman at Jacob's well. This is a violation of the religious taboo against sharing a vessel with a Samaritan woman, who was regarded as unclean. The woman registers surprise: "How is it that You, being a Jew, ask me for a drink since I am a Samaritan woman?" His disciples are similarly "amazed" to come upon him in the midst of this conversation with an untouchable (John 4:5–42). Jesus' attitudes toward women were notably "modern" and advanced, a point also illustrated in the synoptic gospels. In the story of the sisters Mary and Martha, Mary is portrayed as absorbed in Jesus' discussion of spiritual matters, while Martha plays the traditional role of preparing an elaborate supper. When Martha complains of her sister, Jesus reproves Martha, indicating that there was no reason to prepare an elaborate meal ("only one thing is necessary"), that this was her choice, and that her sister Mary had "chosen the good part, which shall not be taken away from her" (Luke 10:38–42).[21] (Jesus' attitudes toward women were also a good deal more advanced than Paul's, whose culturally saturated views of women's subordinate role in public worship prevailed in Christian thinking for most of the past two thousand years.)

The message of ethnic and cultural tolerance continues through the text narrating the history of the early Church, the Acts of the Apostles. Interestingly, perhaps a majority of miracles or acts of divine intervention recounted in the Acts are aimed at instructing the early Christians on the necessity of ethnic and cultural tolerance. The message begins with the miracle of Pentecost, where after being imbued with the Holy Spirit, the apostles address a multiethnic, multilingual crowd of "Jews and proselytes" in Jerusalem—"Parthians and Medes and Elamites, residents of . . . Phrygia and Pampuylia, Egypt . . . Cretans and Arabs." Each is said to hear what is said in his own language: "And how is it that we each hear them in our own language to which we were born?" (Acts 2:7–11). The miracle of the "tongues" adumbrates the multiethnic nature of the new religious outlook.[22]

Christianity was from the start a self-consciously multi-cultural, multiethnic religion, and in this sense unique.[23] As is clear from the Acts narrative, the major challenge of the earliest Church was precisely the overcoming of ethnic and cultural divisions, between Palestinian and Hellenized Jews, between Jews and Samaritans, and above all between Jews and Gentiles, with whom Jews were forbidden to eat or associate on grounds that Gentiles were ritually "un-clean" (even more so than Samaritans). Peter, the leading apostle, is given a vision of animals descending from heaven on a sheet. He is instructed to "kill and eat." He re-fuses three times, on grounds of religious dietary laws, and is finally told, "What God has cleansed no longer consider unholy." This prepares him for his first (also divinely arranged) encounter with a Gentile, the centurion Cornelius, whom he dines with, lodges, and eventually baptizes. The apostles are astonished to witness Cornelius inspired by the Holy Spirit, and Peter arrives at a new recognition: "You yourselves know how unlawful it is for a man who is a Jew to associate with a foreigner or to visit him; and yet God has shown me that I should not call any man unholy or unclean" (Acts 10). The divine recruitment of Paul on the (now proverbial) road to Damascus is aimed at overcoming ethnic differences: "Saul, Saul, why are you *persecuting* Me?" says the voice of Christ from heaven after Paul is struck off his horse and blinded (Acts 9:1–9). Paul, one of the most intellectual and prominent Pharisaic Jews of his era (his writings remain among the best scholarly sources for the thinking of first-century Pharisaic Judaism),[24] becomes the "apostle to the Gentiles" and battles with the leaders of the Church in Jerusalem to remove circumcision as a requirement for Christian conversion. In yet another miraculous event, the evangelist Philip is led by an angel to an Ethiopian official, whom he evangelizes—indicating the barriers of race, too, must be overcome (Acts 8:26–40). The first community of believers to describe themselves as "Christians" was an interethnic community of Greeks, Jews, and others in Antioch (Acts 11:26). The message of the essential dignity of the human being regardless of race, ethnicity, culture, gender, or social rank is close to the core meaning of original Christianity. As Paul writes to the Galatians, "There is neither Jew nor Greek, there is neither slave nor free, there is neither male nor female; for you are all one in Christ Jesus" (Galatians 3:28).[25]

A MORAL REVOLUTION

We should point out how radically novel these ideas were in human history. To be sure, the Greek philosophers developed a universal idea of "man" that saw the irrelevance of cultural and ethnic standards. It was this philosophical universalism that ultimately underlay both the culturally syncretic Hellenic empire and the later expansion of Roman citizenship to non-Roman cities and individuals. But as free as philosophical universalism might have been from cultural prejudice, it was deeply hierarchical in its view of the human being, when it came to class and gender as well as intellect, beauty, and other qualities and talents. It divided human beings not so much by culture as into categories of "high" and "low." Citizenship in the ancient world was more in the nature of a privilege than a right, something that differentiated a "gentleman" from inferiors; women were, of course, denied political participation, and slaves were legally defined as property or chattel. (Notably, crucifixion was a form of punishment generally not suffered by Roman citizens and normally reserved for slaves.)[26] In the doctrine of the Greek philosophers, perhaps not surprisingly, the philosopher was understood as the highest and best man who had a "natural" right to rule over his less intelligent fellow citizens.

Even more important, the classical philosophers' ideas of virtue, as is well known, were radically at odds with those of Christianity. They viewed compassion as a sign of weakness and humility as the embodiment of contemptibility. The most "virtuous" man, according to Aristotle, was the man with a "great soul" who "thinks he deserves great things and actually deserves them." Modesty and humility were far from virtues;

they indicated *mikropsychia*, or a "small soul": "A man who underestimates himself is small-minded [that is, literally, "small-souled"] regardless of whether his worth is great or moderate, or whether it is small and he thinks it is smaller still."[27] For Aristotle and the Greek philosophers generally, the "worth" of a human being could be ranked; some people were simply worth more than others—notably the intelligent, the beautiful, the proud, and so forth. Moreover, after philosophy, or intelligence, pride was the core virtue of the classical philosophical outlook, the "crown of the virtues."[28]

When Jesus begins the Sermon on the Mount with the statement "Blessed are the poor in spirit" (Matthew 5:3), he is flying in the face of this classical worldview and, of course, of the views of "this world" generally. Indeed, as the atheist philosopher Nietzsche recognized, the essential logic of classical virtue was radically this-worldly, not surprisingly, since it was based purely on reasoning about the material and human world. In the classical understanding, the strong, the beautiful, the intelligent, the rich were not just better off but *morally* better than the weak, the poor, the meek, the downtrodden. That is why Nietzsche, in some ways the embodiment of the Satanic voice in modern philosophy (even by his own definition!),[29] identified the rise of Christianity in the ancient world as a fundamental moral revolution and the triumph of what he called "slave morality."[30]

All of our most modern ideas about humaneness, kindness, and charity, about ethnic, cultural, and religious tolerance, and about the essential dignity of the human being—regardless of race, gender, abilities, or station—originated in the New Testament. This is not to say that they are the exclusive preserve of Christianity—or even that they have been practiced by

Christianity or Christians more than by other religions or peoples. Such values lie at the core of every major religion. (As Gandhi said, "If a man goes to the heart of his own religion, he has reached to the heart of the others, too.")[31] But as a purely historical matter, the New Testament is the point where these values entered the bloodstream of human history, where the vision appeared with a wholeness and emphasis capable of transforming the nature of human societies. That this transformation has taken two thousand years and is still far from complete should not be surprising, given what we know about the nature of human beings, given what a scientist might attribute to biology and a Christian to "sin."

TWO SIDES OF THE ENLIGHTENMENT

It is often said that modern ideas of tolerance originated with the Enlightenment, the rebirth of reason in Western thinking. There is truth in this, but it is a half truth. The Enlightenment had two distinct sides—a "light" and a very "dark" one. In some sense, the history of the twentieth century has been the dramatic confrontation between the Enlightenment's two faces. To credit the Enlightenment with all that is "enlightened" about the modern outlook is no more accurate than to credit the historical Christian religion with all that was good or humane in history. To quote Gandhi again, "much of what passes as Christianity is a negation of the Sermon on the Mount."[32] As best as we can tell, the very early Church, the pre-imperial Church, embodied the New Testament values to a remarkable degree. Christianity gained converts in the ancient world with extraordinary rapidity.[33] If we are to credit the early Church texts (and Luke, the author of the Acts of the Apostles, strikes the reader as a level-headed, reliable narrator), part of the reason for this rapid growth was the miracles or "signs and wonders" that marked early Christian life—miraculous healings, visions, and so forth. This moment in history seems to have been marked by an unusual interpenetration of the human with the divine. But part of the reason for Christianity's rapid spread, historians have remarked, was simply that the early Christians were such nice people. The very kindness of the Christians and their service to the poor and downtrodden attracted new adherents. "Christians astounded the ancients with their charity," as one historian has put it.[34] Christianity spread partially by proselytization and partially by pure example. To put it in today's jargon, the early Christians "walked their talk." But the bigger Christianity became, the more bureaucratic it grew. The Edict of Milan, which made Christianity the official religion of the Empire, was a great boon for the Church and a historical guarantee that Christianity would shape the West. But, as has often been observed, it also led to a politicization of the Church, a partial resubmersion, as it were, of spirituality in culture. Gandhi, a Hindu who learned profoundly from Jesus but who had many bad experiences with Christians, wrote in the 1930s, when Britain still ruled India, that when Christianity "had the backing of a Roman Emperor it became an imperialist faith as it remains to this day."[35] One could hardly quarrel with him.

By the Middle Ages the Church was hardly distinguishable from any other political entity. The pope ruled the papal states, vied in secular power struggles, and even rallied Christians to war—including, of course, the Crusades, in which Christians slaughtered Muslims as a way of witnessing to their faith. (Can anyone imagine Jesus' displeasure at such behavior?) The Inquisition burned witches and heretics and persecuted independent thinkers. The bloody persecution of Jews was a recurrent phenomenon. The great legacy of the Renaissance, Reformation, and Enlightenment was the destruction of the Church's political power and the freeing of the human intellect from politically driven religious restraint. Of course, leave it to human beings to turn liberation into a new round of tribalism, as the supposed reformers waged war on the unreformed, and vice versa.

But I have said that the Enlightenment, or more generally, the rebirth of reason in Western culture, had both a "good" and a "bad" side. This is an important dimension of modern history that has often been overlooked, especially by contemporary admirers of Enlightenment thinking. As a historical matter, reason did not free human beings from dogmatism or tribalism or the worst cruelties—as we have witnessed firsthand well into our own century. The rational or "scientific" faith of Marxist-Leninist ideology sanctioned cruelties of a type and on a scale hardly imagined by the Inquisition in its darkest hours. Some estimates place the number of victims of Soviet Communism as high as 60 million, and the methods of torture employed by the Soviet regime marked a kind of "progress" in this cruel art.[36] Moreover, scientific rationalism, ironically, became the basis of the most absurd form of dogma and dogmatism that history records—the "scientific" ideology of Marxism-Leninism.

Similar things can be said, of course, of Nazism, which was less a form of atheism than a quasi-mystical antireligion, or religion of evil, with its own dark symbolism and neopagan myth and ritual.[37] In addition to his major project of exterminating Jews (along with Gypsies, Jehovah's Witnesses, the mentally retarded, and other groups), Hitler sought to destroy the mainstream churches. Hundreds of priests and nuns were sent to concentration camps.[38] The Hitler Youth were indoctrinated in blasphemy. At the 1934 Nuremberg Party rally, the Hitler Youth sang that they were "children of Hitler," a blasphemous parody of "children of God": "No evil priest can prevent us from feeling that we are the children of Hitler. We follow not Christ but Horst Wessel. Away with incense and holy water. The church can go hang for all we care. The Swastika brings salvation on earth."[39] Orphans in state-controlled orphanages said a new grace before meals and sang a Nazi version of the favorite German Christmas carol, "Silent Night," in which Hitler took the place of God and baby Jesus.[40] The regime even developed neopagan marriage and baptismal ceremonies, which were practiced by the SS and their families.[41] The racist Aryan movement of the early twentieth century had a large occult dimension, which Hitler may have had at least a glancing encounter with in his Vienna days.[42]

The interesting thing is that the "good" and "bad" sides of the Enlightenment legacy have tracked very closely, historically, with the absence or prevalence of atheism, or an anti-God point of view. This was apparent in the contrast between the first two great revolutions produced by Enlightenment thinking—the American and the French—and noticed at the time. There is a contemporary debate between evangelical Christians and secular historians about the role of religion in America's founding.[43] By and large, evangelicals who argue that America's founding was dominantly religious in character vastly overstate their case. Much of the thinking behind the framing of the American regime was secular or deistic in character—notably, Jefferson's. The Framers made ample use of the insights of modern philosophers, many of whom were atheists or at least nonbelievers. But at the same time, the thinking behind America's founding was not antireligious or anti-God in any dimension. Many, perhaps most, who migrated from Europe to America came wholly or partly for religious reasons—usually to avoid persecution—up to and including my Catholic Irish grandparents, who fled the partly religiously justified rigors of British rule in Ireland. America was from the start, and remains, a deeply religious country. More pertinent, the Framers included both eighteenth-century deists and pious believers. There was a consensus on restraining religion in politics—indeed, religious persecution was one of the major problems that the American regime was designed to solve—but no desire to destroy religion; in fact, there was broad recognition of its necessity to society.[44] The founding document of the regime—the Declaration of Independence—invoked the "Creator" as justification for human rights. Even if this word was written by Jefferson in a deistic spirit, it reflected what he understood to be the fundamentally religious orientation of his civilization. Early American society was steeped in religion; the Continental Congress repeatedly declared days of prayer and fasting throughout the Revolutionary War.[45] Leaders such as George Washington and Benjamin Franklin had a strong belief in divine "Providence" or guidance of human affairs.[46]

All this was in sharp contrast with the French Revolution, which, as Edmund Burke noticed at the time, was inspired by the purest atheism.[47] That is perhaps one reason why the main memory of this event, to recall George Orwell's phrase, is of "a pyramid of severed heads." The French Revolution, in contrast to the American one, led to political cruelty on a scale that Europe had not before seen. This is not to deny that there may be a plethora of purely historical reasons why these two revolutions took different courses. The Americans, for one thing, had a vastly simpler task—a new country and a mostly clean slate to draw on. But there is an interesting historical correlation between atheism, on the one hand, and moral and political catastrophe, on the other hand, that has extended on up into our own time. We sometimes forget that the twentieth century saw the first large-scale, long-term human experiment with a state based entirely on atheistic principles—the Soviet Union—and the result on every front was unmitigated disaster.

THE POSTSECULAR MOMENT

The very collapse of Communism belongs to what I would call the present postsecular moment, for human spirituality played a unique and pivotal role in Communism's defeat. This is rarely acknowledged. To be sure, secular historians would say that the greatest mistake of Communism was to attempt to defy the laws of economics. But other laws, too, came into play. The most potent internal challenge to Communism in the 1980s was Poland's religiously steeped Solidarity movement (which had the backing of the Polish pope). Without Catholic Solidarity and the Lutheran-inspired "Revolution of Light" in East Germany, it is unlikely that Communism would have fallen or fallen peacefully. Moreover, as historians penetrate the circumstances of the Communist collapse, it is becoming clearer that the Soviet elite was itself in the throes of an atheistic "crisis of faith." Having lived under an atheistic ideology—one that consisted of lies and that was based on a "Big Lie"—the Soviet system suffered a radical demoralization, in every sense of that term. People, including the ruling elite, lost all sense of morality and all sense of hope.[48] It is ever clearer in retrospect that Mikhail Gorbachev's perception of the failures of his system was in large measure a moral perception, a perception that society had lost touch with morality at every level. His initial approach to reform focused on a moral problem—alcoholism. He described what he saw as the sources of his society's crisis in his January 1987 speech to the Plenum of the Communist Party:

> Interest in the affairs of society slackened, manifestations of callousness and skepticism appeared and the role of moral incentives to work declined. The stratum of people, some of them young people, whose ultimate goal in life was material well-being and gain by any means, grew wider. Their cynical stand was acquiring more and more aggressive forms, poisoning the mentality of those around them. . . .
>
> Disregard for laws, report-padding, bribe-taking and encouragement of toadyism and adulation had a deleterious influence on the moral atmosphere in society. Real care for people, for the conditions of their life and work and for social well-being were often replaced with political flirtation—the mass distribution of awards, titles and prizes. An atmosphere of permissiveness was taking shape, exactingness, discipline and responsibility were declining.[49]

The crisis that Gorbachev saw, in short, was a moral and spiritual one. At first, he tried to remoralize his society by returning to the ideological roots of Marxism-Leninism, to the inspiring figure of Lenin.[50] Later, incongruously, the Soviet leader began to refer on certain occasions to "God."[51] Those who knew the Soviet Union from the inside—for example Aleksandr Solzhenitsyn—recognized that the system's crisis was primarily a moral and spiritual one.[52] Even Western social scientists had begun to notice curious symptoms of decline—for example, Communist societies in Europe, alone among industrial countries, appeared to have increasing mortality rates, doubtless a product of wide-scale alcoholism and related problems that could be interpreted as symptoms of psychological demoralization, related in turn to a banishment of spirituality from life.[53] Most experts that I know (and in my work in arms control I have had the opportunity to participate in discussions with many of the most prominent of them) still regard the collapse of Soviet Communism as fundamentally a mystery. I would suggest that part of this mystery may be explained by purely spiritual factors—an argument put forth forcefully in George Weigel's excellent book *The Final Revolution*.[54]

We have seen the mischievous consequences of atheistically inspired social policy and social experimentation closer to home. The philosophical underpinnings of the sexual revolution of the 1960s and 1970s were essentially atheistic and antireligious, though based avowedly on "science." As we have seen already, there is now a growing consensus in society, even among secular scholars, that this revolution has created vastly more harm than good—whether measured by an explosion in teenage pregnancies and out-of-wedlock births, a skyrocketing divorce rate and the often-related problems of juvenile delinquency and teen-age suicide, or the epidemic of sexually transmitted diseases.[55] Most of this sexual experimentation originated in America's own brief "death of God" phase.

(When *Time* magazine, reflecting the prevailing secular turn of the era, emblazoned on its cover in 1966 the question "Is God Dead?" it was an ill omen for American society if ever there was one.)[56] An interesting and representative example of that era's thinking was the book *Open Marriage: A New Life Style for Couples,* by anthropologists Nena and George O'Neill, which marshaled the latest social theories to preach the supposed benefits to a marriage if both partners agree to permit each other to engage in extramarital sex. "The patriarchal marriage system of the Judeo-Christian tradition, based on an agrarian economy, is simply outmoded today," announced the authors in a book that was a national bestseller in 1972.[57] Five years later, Nena O'Neill essentially recanted, revealing that numerous couples whom the pair studied had—not surprisingly, perhaps—found the experiment in consensual adultery disastrous.[58]

Modern social science now "knows" why the O'Neills were wrong. It has the data to demonstrate the ill consequences of the sexual permissiveness preached by an earlier generation of social thinkers. But for social science to have discovered, two thousand years after the birth of Christ, that divorce is a bad thing and religious faith is generally beneficial to people does not bespeak a great advance in human understanding.

A final sobering lesson of our century concerns the degree to which reason is ruled by preconceptions, not only in the social sciences, but even in the physical ones. "Positivists" of Bertrand Russell's day assumed that reason decisively freed the mind from dogmatism, since its method was "piecemeal" and "cautious." It built up the truth gradually, from particular observations and experiments. That was its decisive advantage over the religious outlook. "The way in which science arrives at its beliefs is quite different," he wrote, "from that of medieval theology. . . . Science starts, not from large assumptions, but from particular facts discovered by observation or experiment."[59] But research in the history and sociology of science has shown that this is far from the being the case. As Thomas Kuhn demonstrated in his groundbreaking work on the structure of scientific revolutions, "normal science," or the work of reason, is always guided by some larger insight or belief—what Kuhn called a "paradigm."[60] Confronted with anomalous evidence that fails to fit the reigning "paradigm," scientists do not typically let go of their accustomed model. Rather, their impulse is invariably to deny the evidence or explain it away. The great advances of science occur through "revolutions," in which proponents of a new paradigm struggle with the adherents of an old one. Einstein himself was on the defensive side of such a battle; having discovered relativity, he could not accept the implications of quantum mechanics and proposed extremely clever counterexamples. The battle was only completely resolved by an experiment in the early 1980s, long after Einstein had died.[61] Though reasoning, observation, and experiment lie at the heart of science, the greatest scientific progress often seems to come from intuitive leaps. "Positivism"—the confidence that reason alone could defeat dogmatism—has gone the way of the century's other atheistic doctrines, adding its weight to what Marx called "the ash-heap of history." Reason has proved an imperfect guide to the ultimate truths about the physical world, let alone the ultimate truths about the universe and human life.

REASON AND SPIRIT

What I am suggesting, and what it seems to me history tends to corroborate, is this: The knowledge of Spirit is prior to the knowledge of reason. Where reason follows Spirit, the results are good; where it rejects or parts ways with Spirit, the results are invariably disastrous, whether one speaks of the political, societal, or personal spheres. Reason rediscovers and reconstructs in slow, cumbersome, linear, and partial fashion what Spirit already knows. There is nothing morally or socially admirable about the post-Enlightenment world that does not go back to values that were given to humankind whole in a priori form in the New Testament. Jesus already "knew" what modern humanity has only painstakingly discovered after two thousand years, and has yet to fully learn. The great achievement of the Enlightenment was, through the use of reason and common sense, to construct political and social institutions that would make the kind of respect for dignity of the individual human being that Jesus taught us a political reality in much of the developed world. These political institutions went a long way toward helping human beings free themselves from a tribalism that the Gospel already condemned. The reason we admire what we admire in the modern polity is precisely that the values Jesus put forward in the New Testament are the central human values, and God has imprinted them on our souls. This knowledge lies deeper and is larger than reason, and one of the human tasks is to recover it. But reason is strongest, as was true for so many of our forefathers, when it accepts divine guidance.[62]

Reason is not a source of value; it is not by itself a reliable guide to the right or the good. History shows: It does not free the mind of dogmatism. It does not free the mind of prejudice. It does not free the mind of cruelty. It is a logical and calculative function of the brain that is tied to the slowness of our biology and the material world. What we all have "upstairs" is a "slow CPU" that cannot grasp the whole truth, which exists a priori in a spiritual realm and which has been revealed to us at moments of extraordinary interpenetration of the divine with the human world. Using our "slow CPU," we can occasionally capture pieces of the truth, in fragmentary form. But left to its own, used in a spirit unrelated to Spirit, this slow CPU will lead us straight to disaster, as experience shows.

The great error of the Enlightenment—for which the worst horrors of modern history are themselves the evidence—was the idolatry of reason, the belief that reason could replace God. Marx was such an idolater. Freud was another. The latter spoke, in *The Future of an Illusion*, of our "God *logos*"—that is, reason.[63] Is it any wonder that the Communist experiment eventuated in disaster or that a later generation of scholars has concluded that Freud's views of religion and of a thousand other aspects of human psychology were wrongheaded? Should we be surprised that "godless Communism" resulted in unprecedented cruelties or that "godless psychiatry" has come under increasing criticism in recent years for condoning self-evidently immoral behavior?

But doesn't the suggestion that Spirit is prior to reason threaten to drive us back into a state of primitive ignorance and superstition or, worse, forward into a world of postmodern irrationality, where cultists might claim spiritual insights that lead them to mass suicides and other forms of madness? We saw that reason, in the end, afforded no protection against social madness—human beings, we have found in this century, kill as readily in the service of a "rational" dogmatism as a religious one and, perhaps in the end, more readily. If reason, in the final analysis, offers no protection against evil, then are we helpless in the face of our ignorance? There is in fact a simple test of insights, one that Jesus offers in the New Testament and that we tend to apply in practice anyway: "You will know them by their fruits" (Matthew 7:16). Such was Jesus' advice in dealing with the problem of "false prophets"—and it might be applied as easily to the prophets of the "god" of reason as to the prophets of any cult. We certainly could see the fruits of Communism. The fruits of religious intolerance in places like Northern Ireland or the Balkans are obvious enough. It is not a difficult thing for human beings to judge whether the consequences of a particular line of thinking or a particular approach to life are good or bad. But this presumes that our moral perception, our ability to distinguish good from evil, is prior to our rational understanding. It seems to me that such a conclusion is inescapable. Without an ability to distinguish right from wrong, life degenerates rapidly into a tale told by an idiot. All of us of course have the ability to distinguish right from wrong, but sometimes this moral sense is clouded over, by what the biblical tradition calls "sin." All of us have had this experience, and all of us have seen others in the grip of such confusion, people who are rationalizing bad decisions, immoral decisions, that we know will lead them and others in their lives only to pain and suffering. When others do this, it is painfully obvious, even if we can be slow to recognize such wrongheadedness in ourselves. There is a close and inescapable connection between wisdom and goodness. Only people with relatively clear consciences are capable of distinguishing good and evil with clarity; and only people who are capable of distinguishing between good and evil with clarity are capable of making sound decisions or, for that matter, constructing sound theories on subjects pertaining to politics, psychology, sociology, and other aspects of human moral life.

The moral law is no secret to humanity. God is beyond our comprehension, but His commandments are not. Nor is there great variance in these commandments among the world's great religions—particular ritual practices and prohibitions vary, but there is little variance in the basic moral law as understood by Christians, Jews, Muslims, Hindus, Buddhists, or anybody else. One of the more interesting developments in the realm of theology in recent years has been the growing body of work demonstrating the broad agreement among the various religious traditions on fundamental moral issues.[64] In 1993, partly under the impetus of theologian Hans Küng, representatives of the world's religions gathered in Chicago for a "Parliament" that produced in turn a declaration. The declaration set forth a series of obvious moral precepts, ranging from noting the evil of sexual immorality on up to the crimes of murder and genocide. This consensual document represented agreement among an extraordinarily large and varied number of religious perspectives. While each tradition would probably ask more of its adherents than the document contained, the moral vision set forth in this consensus statement was remarkably rich.[65] Right and wrong are no secret to us—until we begin to deny that they exist. If the history of this century offers any lesson, it is that goodness—and a relationship to God, to the Absolute by whatever name He is called—is not only the beginning of wisdom but the only path by which it can be attained.

Notes

Introduction

1. According to various Gallup surveys, 94 percent of Americans believe in God and 90 percent pray. Seventy-one percent say they believe in life after death; only 16 percent say they do not. George Gallup, Jr., and Jim Catelli, *The People's Religion: American Faith in the 90's* (New York: Macmillan, 1989), pp. 45, 58.
2. Harvey Cox, *The Secular City* (New York: Macmillan, 1965).
3. "Is God Dead?" *Time*, April 8, 1966.
4. J. Hillis Miller, *The Disappearance of God* (Cambridge: Harvard University Press, 1963).
5. Bertrand Russell, *Religion and Science* (London: Oxford University Press, 1961; originally published 1935), p. 222.
6. Socrates was known by his contemporaries to be an atheist, as indicated by the comedies of Aristophanes, especially *The Clouds*. For a useful brief treatment of this subject, see Thomas G. West and Grace Starry West, eds., *Four Texts on Socrates* (Ithaca: Cornell University Press, 1984), esp. pp. 31–32 and 125 n49. On the general link between the rise of classical philosophy and the critique of religious belief or "convention," see Leo Strauss,

Natural Right and History (Chicago: University of Chicago Press, 1953), esp. pp. 81–100. It was Strauss who rediscovered the essentially antireligious thrust of classical philosophy, though he attempted to imitate Plato in keeping "esoteric," or secret, this radically antireligious viewpoint. See Leo Strauss, *Persecution and the Art of Writing* (Chicago: University of Chicago Press, 1980), pp. 22–37. On Shakespeare's Platonism and familiarity with the Platonic tradition, see Paul A. Cantor, *Shakespeare's Rome: Republic and Empire* (Ithaca: Cornell University Press, 1976), pp. 10, 14, 113–114, 145, 213 n17, 216 n17, 217 n20, 220–221 n18; and Allan Bloom, with Harry Jaffa, *Shakespeare's Politics* (Chicago: University of Chicago Press, 1981), esp. pp. 76–83, 144 n35. On Shakespeare's skeptical view of Christian beliefs, see Paul A. Cantor, ed., *Shakespeare, Hamlet* (Cambridge: Cambridge University Press, 1989), pp. 20, 40–53. The problem of Socrates' students turning on Athenian democracy is discussed in West and West, pp. 84–85; see also Christopher Bruell, "Xenophon," in Leo Strauss and Joseph Cropsey, eds., *History of Political Philosophy*, 3rd ed. (Chicago: University of Chicago Press, 1987), pp. 103–107. See also the further discussion in this chapter and in Chapter 5.

7. Edwin R. Wallace IV, "Psychiatry and Religion: A Dialogue," in Joseph H. Smith and Susan A. Handelman, eds., *Psychoanalysis and Religion* (Baltimore: Johns Hopkins University Press, 1990), p. 105.

8. Ephesians 2:8.

9. Paul A. Cantor, "Leo Strauss and Contemporary Hermeneutics," in Alan Udoff, ed., *Leo Strauss's Thought* (Boulder: Lynne Reinner, 1991), pp. 267–274; and see note 6 above.

10. Strauss saw the vision of the Greek philosophers, which he embraced, as "diametrically opposed" to the biblical one, as he

wrote to Eric Voegelin in 1951. His quarrel with Voegelin was in response to the latter's wish to see the Greek philosophers as "proto-Christians," or nascently mystical and monotheistic thinkers. Strauss firmly disagreed with this. He absolutely insisted on the recognition of classical philosophy as a radical critique of religion, indeed *the* critique of religion. By implication, this made philosophy a viewpoint deeply atheistic in spirit, though Strauss would never have said so openly. Where he differed from many Western scholars was in seeing the Socratic critique of religion as valid in principle not just vis-à-vis Greek polytheism, but also vis-à-vis Judeo-Christian monotheism. Peter Emberley and Barry Cooper, eds., *Faith and Political Philosophy: The Correspondence Between Leo Strauss and Eric Voegelin, 1934–1964* (University Park: Pennsylvania State University Press, 1993), esp. pp. 78–79, also 326–327, 344; and Alan Udoff, "On Leo Strauss: An Introductory Account," in Udoff, *Leo Strauss's Thought*, pp. 14–15. Strauss modeled his attitude toward American democracy on that of Socrates toward Athenian democracy, described in Leo Strauss, *The City and Man* (Chicago: University of Chicago Press, 1964), pp. 131–134. A defense and description of the Straussian movement is to be found in Hadley Arkes, "Strauss and the Religion of Reason," *National Review*, June 26, 1995, pp. 60–63.

11. According to the Straussian formula, and following the practice of Plato, this view was supposed to be kept more or less a "secret." Perhaps the most open discussion of the issue by a follower of Strauss, employing Strauss's framework, is to be found in Stanley Rosen, *Nihilism: A Philosophical Essay* (New Haven: Yale University Press, 1969), pp. 209–218.

12. Martin Buber, *I and Thou*, tr. Walter Kaufmann (New York: Scribner, 1970), p. 53.

13. Buber, p. 83.
14. Buber, p. 111.
15. Buber, p. 96.
16. George F. Will, *The Pursuit of Virtue and Other Tory Notions* (New York: Simon & Schuster, 1982), pp. 257–258.
17. Buber, p. 123.
18. Buber, pp. 66–67.
19. Michael Novak, *The Spirit of Democratic Capitalism* (New York: Simon and Schuster, 1982), p. 53.

Chapter 1

1. An account of the events relating to Copernicus's birthday can be found in Owen Gingerich, "International Copernican Celebrations in Poland," *Sky and Telescope,* December 1973.
2. Brandon Carter, "Large Number Coincidences and the Anthropic Principle in Cosmology," in M. S. Longair, ed., *Confrontation of Cosmological Theories with Observational Data* (Dordrecht: D. Reidel, 1974), pp. 291–298. On the personal relationship between Carter and Hawking, see Michael White and John Gribbin, *Stephen Hawking: A Life in Science* (New York: Dutton, 1992), pp. 71–72.
3. Carter, p. 291.
4. Bertrand Russell, *Religion and Science* (Oxford: Oxford University Press, 1961; originally published 1935), p. 216.
5. Russell, p. 222.
6. R. H. Dicke, "Dirac's Cosmology and Mach's Principle" [Letters to the Editor], *Nature,* November 4, 1961, pp. 440–441.
7. John Horgan, *The End of Science* (New York: Broadway, 1997), p. 81.

8. Carter, pp. 219–298.

9. Tony Rothman, "A 'What You See Is What You Beget' Theory," *Discover*, May 1987, pp. 90–98.

10. Carter, p. 291.

11. The first important discussion of the anthropic principle in books for general readers did not come until 1988, with the publication of two volumes: Stephen W. Hawking, *A Brief History of Time: From the Big Bang to Black Holes*, intr. Carl Sagan (Toronto: Bantam, 1988), and John D. Barrow and Frank J. Tipler, *The Anthropic Cosmological Principle* (Oxford: Oxford University Press, 1988). The latter volume, a dauntingly thick and technical tome, treated many of the philosophical and theological implications of the idea.

12. John North, *The Norton History of Astronomy and Cosmology* (New York: Norton, 1995), pp. 530–532.

13. North, p. 532.

14. North, pp. 561–563.

15. White and Gribbin, pp. 216–219.

16. Carter, pp. 295–298; cf. John Leslie, *Universes* (London: Routledge, 1989), pp. 37–38.

17. Leslie, p. 5.

18. Leslie, p. 34.

19. Leslie, p. 4.

20. Leslie, pp. 39–40.

21. Barrow and Tipler, pp. 143–144, 524–541. Cf. Denys Wilkinson, *Our Universes* (New York: Columbia University Press, 1991), pp. 171–172.

22. Wilkinson, pp. 181–183; see also John Gribbin and Martin Rees, *Cosmic Coincidences* (New York: Bantam, 1989), pp. 243–247.

23. See note 16.

24. Fred Hoyle, *The Origin of the Universe and the Origin of Religion* (Wakefield, RI: Moyer Bell, 1993), p. 19.

25. Hoyle, p. 18.

26. Cf. Barrow and Tipler, pp. 29–30, 123–218.

27. Aristotle, *Metaphysics* 1013a–1013b.

28. The most balanced and thorough account of the Galileo affair is to be found in Annibale Fantoli, *Galileo: For Copernicanism and for the Church*, 2nd ed., tr. George V. Coyne (Rome: Vatican Observatory Publications; Notre Dame, IN: University of Notre Dame Press, 1996).

29. Richard Westfall, "The Rise of Science and the Decline of Orthodox Christianity," in David C. Lindberg and Ronald L. Numbers, eds., *God and Nature: Historical Essays on the Encounter Between Christianity and Science* (Berkeley: University of California Press, 1986), pp. 224–234. On Descartes, cf. Richard Kennington, "Descartes," in Leo Strauss and Joseph Cropsey, eds., *History of Political Philosophy*, 2nd ed. (Chicago: University of Chicago Press, 1972), pp. 395–396, 400–401, 403–405.

30. Basil Willey, *The Eighteenth Century Background* (London: Chatto & Windus, 1946), pp. 3–13.

31. Ernst Cassirer, *The Philosophy of the Enlightenment*, tr. Fritz C. A. Koelln and James P. Pettegrove (Princeton: Princeton University Press, 1951), pp. 134–196.

32. Charles Coulston Gillispie, *Genesis and Geology* (Cambridge: Harvard University Press, 1951), pp. 98–103, 121–147.

33. Augustine wrote, "Usually, even a non-Christian knows something about the earth, the heavens, and the other elements of this world, about the motion and orbit of the stars and even their size and relative positions, about the predictable eclipses of

the sun and moon, the cycles of the years and the seasons, about the kinds of animals, shrubs, stones, and so forth, and this knowledge he holds to as being certain from reason and experience. Now, it is a disgraceful and dangerous thing for an infidel to hear a Christian, presumably giving the meaning of Holy Scripture, talking nonsense on these topics; and we should take all means to prevent such an embarrassing situation, in which people show up vast ignorance in a Christian and laugh it to scorn. The shame is not so much that an ignorant individual is derided, but that people outside the household of faith think our sacred writers held such opinions, and, to the great loss of those for whose salvation we toil, the writers of our Scripture are criticized and rejected as unlearned men. If they find a Christian mistaken in a field which they themselves know well and hear him maintaining his foolish opinions about our books, how are they going to believe those books in matters concerning the resurrection of the dead, the hope of eternal life, and the kingdom of heaven, when they think their pages are full of falsehoods on facts which they themselves have learnt from experience and the light of reason? Reckless and incompetent expounders of Holy Scripture bring untold trouble and sorrow on their wiser brethren when they are caught in one of their mischievous false opinions and are taken to task by those who are not bound by the authority of our sacred books. For then, to defend their utterly foolish and obviously untrue statements, they will try to call upon Holy Scripture for proof and even recite from memory many passages which they think support their position, although *they understand neither what they say nor the things about which they make assertion.*" Augustine, *The Literal Meaning of Genesis*, tr. John Hammond Taylor, *Ancient*

Christian Writers: The Works of the Fathers in Translation, no. 41 (New York: Newman Press, 1982), vol. 1, pp. 42–43.

34. See Walter E. Houghton, *The Victorian Frame of Mind 1830–1870* (New Haven: Yale University Press, 1973), pp. 58–77.

35. Quoted in Houghton, p. 238.

36. Quoted in Hans Küng, *Freud and the Problem of God,* enlarged ed., tr. Edward Quinn (New Haven: Yale University Press, 1990), p. 3.

37. J. Hillis Miller, *The Disappearance of God* (Cambridge, MA: Harvard University Press, 1963).

38. Michael Denton, *Evolution: A Theory in Crisis* (Bethesda, MD: Adler and Adler, 1985), pp. 25–35.

39. Quoted in W. C. Dampier, *A History of Science,* postscript I. Bernard Cohen (Cambridge: Cambridge University Press, 1989), p. 279.

40. Gertrude Himmelfarb, *Darwin and the Darwinian Revolution* (London: Chatto and Windus, 1959), p. 316.

41. Huxley's 1889 essay can be found in Thomas Henry Huxley, *Agnosticism and Christianity* (Buffalo, NY: Prometheus, 1992). On Darwin's use of the term, see Adrian Desmond and James Moore, *Darwin: The Life of a Tormented Evolutionist* (New York: Norton, 1994), p. 636.

42. Walter Kaufmann, ed., *The Viking Portable Nietzsche* (New York: Viking, 1968), p. 124.

43. Paul Davies and John Gribbin, *The Matter Myth* (New York: Simon & Schuster, 1992), p. 10.

44. See, for example, Heinz R. Pagels, "A Cozy Cosmology: The Anthropic Principle Is Convenient, But It's Not Science," *Whole Earth Review,* Summer 1987 pp. 6–12.

45. Lee Smolin, "Did the Universe Evolve?" *Classical and Quantum Gravity* 9 (1992): 174.

46. Leslie, pp. 29–33; Steven Weinberg, "Before the Big Bang," *The New York Review of Books,* June 12, 1997, pp. 19–20.

47. See, for example, Hawking, *A Brief History of Time*, pp. 156, 174–175.

48. Weinberg, p. 20.

49. Quoted in Wilkinson, pp. 188–189.

50. Hawking, *A Brief History of Time*, pp. 140–141.

51. Keith Ward, *Religion and Creation* (Oxford: Clarendon, 1996), p. 299.

52. See, for example, James Glanz, "Debating the Big Questions," *Science*, August 30, 1996.

53. Hoyle made one such prediction using anthropic style reasoning in the 1950s, the anthropic coincidence involving the synthesis of carbon in stars (mentioned in the sixth of the bulleted examples in the text). He realized that a specific resonance would be necessary to synthesize carbon-12 on any significant scale. For life to be possible, such a value would have to exist. He persuaded some reluctant physicists to investigate the matter and was vindicated. Gribbin and Rees, pp. 243–247.

54. James Thrower, *A Short History of Western Atheism* (London: Pemberton, 1971), p. 111.

55. The original context reads: "If an army of monkeys were strumming on typewriters they *might* write all the books in the British Museum. The chance of their doing so is decidedly more favorable than the chance of the molecules returning to one half of the vessel." A. S. Eddington, *The Nature of the Physical World: The Gifford Lectures, 1927* (New York: Macmillan, 1929), p. 72.

56. Immanuel Kant, *Critique of Judgment*, tr. J. H. Bernard (London: Hafner, 1974), esp. pp. 218–222, 149–150.

57. Thomas Kuhn, *The Structure of Scientific Revolutions*, 2nd ed. (Chicago: University of Chicago Press, 1970).

58. Stephen Jay Gould, "Darwinian Fundamentalists," *The New York Review of Books*, June 12, 1997, p. 35.

59. See Richard Dawkins, *The Blind Watchmaker* (New York: Norton, 1986), and Daniel C. Dennett, *Darwin's Dangerous Idea* (New York: Simon & Schuster, 1995).

60. For a clear discussion of the Everett thesis, see Peter Coveney and Roger Highfield, *The Arrow of Time*, foreword Ilya Prigogine (New York: Fawcett, 1990), pp. 129–134.

61. Davies and Gribbin, p. 234.

62. Quoted in P. C. W. Davies and J. R. Brown, *The Ghost in the Atom* (Cambridge: Cambridge University Press, 1993), p. 60.

63. Stephen Hawking, *Black Holes and Baby Universes* (New York: Bantam, 1994).

64. John Gribbin, *Companion to the Cosmos* (Boston: Little, Brown, 1996), p. 25.

65. See Lawrence E. Joseph, *GAIA: The Growth of an Idea* (New York: St. Martin's, 1990). Of course, one cannot exclude that the Gaia hypothesis may one day be proved valid; that is certainly not its scientific status today.

66. John Gribbin, *In the Beginning: After COBE and Before the Big Bang* (Boston: Little, Brown, 1993), pp. 158 ff.; for the Smolin article, see note 45.

67. Smolin, p. 189.

68. Weinberg, p. 19.

69. Russell, p. 13.

70. Smolin, p. 174.

71. See, especially, Paul Davies, *The Mind of God* (New York: Touchstone, 1992), and Paul Davies, *God and the New Physics* (New York: Touchstone, 1983).

72. See, for example, Ted Peters, ed., *Cosmos as Creation* (Nashville: Abingdon, 1989), John Marks Templeton, ed., *Evidence of Purpose* (New York: Continuum, 1994), and Arthur Peacocke, *Theology for a Scientific Age* (Minneapolis: Fortress, 1993).

Chapter 2

1. Sigmund Freud, *The Future of an Illusion*, tr. and ed. James Strachey, intr. Peter Gay (New York: Norton, 1961), pp. 55, 16–21.

2. Edwin R. Wallace IV, "Psychiatry and Religion: A Dialogue," in Joseph H. Smith and Susan A. Handelman, eds., *Psychoanalysis and Religion* (Baltimore: Johns Hopkins University Press, 1990), p. 105.

3. B. F. Skinner, *Beyond Freedom and Dignity* (New York: Knopf, 1971).

4. Albert Ellis, *The Case Against Religion: A Psychotherapist's View* (New York: Institute for Rational Living, 1971). Cf. Mark R. McMinn, *Psychology, Theology, and Spirituality in Christian Counseling* (Wheaton, IL: Tyndale, 1996), p. 4.

5. Quoted in Peter Gay, *A Godless Jew: Freud, Atheism, and the Making of Psychoanalysis* (New Haven: Yale University Press, 1987), p. 81.

6. Quoted in Gay, *A Godless Jew*, p. 18.

7. On the connection between Freud and Feuerbach, see Hans Küng, *Freud and the Problem of God*, enlarged edition, tr. Edward Quinn (New Haven: Yale University Press, 1990), pp. 3–27; on Freud's reading of Nietzsche, see Peter Gay, *Freud:*

A Life for Our Time (New York: Anchor, 1988), pp. 45–46, 128–129, 192, 367.

8. Quoted in Gay, *A Godless Jew,* p. 50.

9. Gay, *A Godless Jew*, p. 3.

10. Gay, *A Godless Jew*, p. 20.

11. Quoted in E. Torrey Fuller, *Freudian Fraud* (New York: HarperPerennial, 1993), p. 15.

12. Nathan G. Hale, Jr., *Freud and the Americans: The Beginnings of Psychoanalysis in the United States, 1876–1917* (New York: Oxford University Press, 1995), pp. 397–433; see also Frederick Lewis Allen, *Only Yesterday: An Informal History of the 1920's* (New York: Harper & Row, 1964), pp. 81, 90–94.

13. Nathan G. Hale, Jr., *The Rise and Crisis of Psychoanalysis in the United States: Freud and the Americans 1917–1985* (New York: Oxford University Press, 1995), pp. 285–286, 293.

14. Lionel Trilling, *The Liberal Imagination* (Harmondsworth, Middlesex, England: Penguin, 1970), p. 46.

15. Philip Rieff, *The Triumph of the Therapeutic: Uses of Faith After Freud* (Harmondsworth, Middlesex, England: Penguin, 1973; originally published 1966).

16. The most comprehensive review of the critical literature on Freud is to be found in Frederick Crews, *The Memory Wars* (New York: New York Review, 1995).

17. David B. Larson, "Have Faith: Religion Can Heal Mental Ills," *Insight on the News*, March 6, 1995, p. 18.

18. A summary of the various studies is to be found in David B. Larson and Susan S. Larson, *The Forgotten Factor in Physical and Mental Health: What Does the Research Show?* Rockville, MD: National Institute for Healthcare Research, 1994.

19. David G. Myers, "Pursuing Happiness," *Psychology Today*, July–August 1993, pp. 32–38.

20. See Küng, *Freud and the Problem of God*, pp. 31–41, 66–75.

21. The most important analyses and critiques of Freud's use and abuse of the scientific method include Allen Esterson, *Seductive Mirage: An Exploration of the Work of Sigmund Freud* (Chicago: Open Court, 1993); Adolf Grünbaum, *The Foundations of Psychoanalysis: A Philosophical Critique* (Berkeley: University of California Press, 1984); and Malcolm MacMillan, *Freud Evaluated: The Completed Arc* (Amsterdam: North-Holland, 1991). Esterson, a mathematician, has written by far the most focused and readable of the three texts. See also Crews, *The Memory Wars*.

22. See Thomas Hobbes, *Leviathan*, ed. C. B. MacPherson (Penguin Books, 1972), pp. 81–83, 689, and cf. discussion in Basil Willey, *The Seventeenth Century Background* (New York: Anchor, 1953), pp. 106–111.

23. See Gay, *A Godless Jew*, pp. 51–53.

24. G. W. Comstock and K. B. Partridge, "Church Attendance and Health," *Journal of Chronic Disease* 25 (1972): 665–672; J. Gartner, D. B. Larson, and G. Allen, "Religious Commitment and Mental Health: A Review of the Empirical Literature," *Journal of Psychology and Theology* 19, no. 1 (1991): 6–25; S. Stack, "The Effect of the Decline in Institutionalized Religion on Suicide, 1954–1978," *Journal for the Scientific Study of Religion* 22 (1983): 239–252. Studies are summarized in Larson and Larson, p. 69.

25. R. B. Loch and R. H. Hughes, "Religion and Youth Substance Abuse," *Journal of Religion and Health* 24, no. 3 (1985): 197–208. Summarized in Larson and Larson, p. 69.

26. Percentages come from D. B. Larson and W. P. Wilson, "Religious Life of Alcoholics," *Southern Medical Journal* 73, no. 6 (1980): 723–727. Numerous additional studies showing a neg-

ative correlation between religious commitment and alcohol abuse are cited in Larson and Larson, pp. 70–71.

27. A 1990 study by Pressman et al., focusing on thirty women age sixty-five or older who underwent hip surgery, found that patients with stronger religious beliefs were less depressed (as indicated by the Geriatric Depression Scale) and recovered from surgery more quickly than their nonbelieving counterparts. P. Pressman, J. S. Lyons, D. B. Larson, and J. J. Strain, "Religious Belief, Depression, and Ambulation Status in Elderly Women with Broken Hips," *American Journal of Psychiatry* 147, no. 6 (1990): 758–760. Four other studies have shown that persons with higher levels of religious commitment are less depressed. Only one study, focusing on adolescents in Tibet, found that religious commitment correlated with higher levels of depression. A longitudinal study of 720 randomly selected adults in metropolitan New Haven found that regular church attenders reported significantly lower levels of psychological distress, regardless of age, education, marital status, or race. More than a dozen other studies have shown a positive correlation between religious commitment and/or church attendance, on the one hand, and greater levels of psychological well-being on the other. Cited in Larson and Larson, pp. 76–81.

28. All five studies on the issue reviewed by Larson and Larson showed a negative correlation between church attendance and divorce. A 1978 study found that church attendance predicted marital satisfaction better than any other variable. N. D. Glenn and C. N. Weaver, "A Multivariate, Multi-Survey Study of Marital Happiness," *Journal of Marriage and the Family* 40 (1978): 269–282. The correlation between church attendance and expressed willingness to marry the same spouse again was found by P. R. Kunz and S. L. Albrecht, "Religion, Marital

Happiness, and Divorce," *International Journal of Sociology of the Family* 7 (1977): 227–232. Cited in Larson and Larson, pp. 73–75.

29. C. Tavris and S. Sadd, *The Redbook Report on Female Sexuality* (New York: Delacorte Press, 1977); cited in Larson and Larson, p. 75.

30. For the Gallup Poll, see David G. Myers, "Pursuing Happiness," *Psychology Today*, July–August 1993, pp. 32–37.

31. Armand M. Nicholi, Jr., "The Adolescent," in Armand M. Nicholi, Jr., ed., *The New Harvard Guide to Psychiatry* (Cambridge: Harvard University Press, 1988), pp. 650–651.

32. See Yale Kramer, "Freud and the Culture Wars, Part 3," *The Public Interest* no. 124 (Summer 1996): 37–52, and notes 12 and 13 above.

33. Nicholi, p. 651.

34. See David B. Larson, James P. Swyers, and Susan S. Larson, *The Costly Consequences of Divorce: Assessing the Clinical, Economic and Public Health Impact of Marital Disruption in the United States.* Rockville, MD: National Institute for Healthcare Research, n.d., pp. 41–88, 107–128.

35. William Doherty, "Bridging Psychotherapy and Moral Responsibility," *The Responsive Community* 5, no. 1 (Winter 1994/95): 43.

36. Quoted in Larson and Larson, p. 81.

37. M. Scott Peck, *Further Along the Road Less Traveled* (New York: Simon & Schuster, 1993), pp. 137–139.

38. Erich Fromm, *Psychoanalysis and Religion* (New Haven: Yale University Press, 1978; originally published 1950); and Erich Fromm, *The Art of Loving* (New York: Harper, 1956).

39. Viktor E. Frankl, *Man's Search for Meaning: An Introduction to Logotherapy*, part one, tr. Ilse Lasch, preface by Gordon W.

Allport, 3rd ed. (New York: Simon & Schuster, 1984; originally published 1963).

40. Abraham H. Maslow, *Religions, Values, and Peak-Experiences* (Columbus: Ohio State University Press, 1964).

41. M. Scott Peck, *The Road Less Traveled* (New York: Simon & Schuster, 1978).

42. M. Scott Peck, *People of the Lie: The Hope for Healing Human Evil* (New York: Simon and Schuster, 1983).

43. See, for example, Beverly Flanigan and James Mauro, "War Crimes of the Heart," *Psychology Today*, September–October 1992, pp. 36–45; M. Scott Peck, *Further Along the Road Less Traveled*, pp. 29–46.

44. Daniel Goleman, "Therapists See Religion as Aid, Not Illusion," *New York Times*, September 10, 1991, p. C1. Cited in Larson and Larson, pp. 63–64.

45. Telephone interview with Connie McCoy, Director of Marketing, New Life Clinics, April 10, 1996.

46. Lewis M. Andrews, "Religion's Challenge to Psychology," *The Public Interest*, no. 120 (Summer 1995): 79–89.

47. Martin E. P. Seligman, *Learned Optimism* (New York: Alfred A. Knopf, 1991), pp. 5, 40–43, 77–79, 99.

48. Billy Graham, *Angels: God's Secret Agents* (Dallas: Word, 1986), p. 149.

49. Seligman, *Learned Optimism*, pp. 203–204, 285.

50. "Bill W. at Guest House," transcription of a talk given by the founder of Alcoholics Anonymous in the late 1960s; available at a number of World Wide Web sites, including *www.ameritech .net/users/clarks/gsttalk.htm*.

51. Blaise Pascal, *Pensées*, tr. John Warrington (New York: Dent, 1960); excerpted in Jacob Needleman, A. K. Bierman, and

James Gould, eds., *Religion for a New Generation,* 2nd ed. (New York: Macmillan, 1977), pp. 524–526.

52. Friedrich Nietzsche, *Beyond Good and Evil,* tr. Walter Kaufmann (New York: Vintage Books, 1966), especially sections 257 and following.

Chapter 3

1. Claudia Wallis, "Faith and Healing," *Time,* June 24, 1996, p. 61.

2. Herbert Benson, with Marg Stark, *Timeless Healing* (New York: Simon & Schuster, 1996), pp. 193–213.

3. G. W. Comstock and K. B. Partridge, "Church Attendance and Health," *Journal of Chronic Disease* 25 (1972): 665–672; cited in David B. Larson and Susan S. Larson, *The Forgotten Factor in Physical and Mental Health: What Does the Research Show?* Rockville, MD: National Institute for Healthcare Research, pp. 111–112.

4. D. B. Larson et al., "The Impact of Religion on Men's Blood Pressure," *Journal of Religion and Health* 28, no. 4 (1989): pp. 265–278; cited in Larson and Larson, pp. 115–118.

5. Larson et al., "The Impact of Religion on Men's Blood Pressure."

6. J. S. Levin and P. L. Schiller, "Is There a Religious Factor in Health?" *Journal of Religion and Health* 26, no. 1 (1989): 9–35; cited in Larson and Larson, p. 120.

7. K. F. Ferraro and C. M. Albrecht-Jensen, "Does Religion Influence Adult Health?" *Journal for the Scientific Study of Religion* 30, no. 2 (1991): 193–202; cited in Larson and Larson, pp. 122–124.

8. Kevin Culligan, "Spirituality and Healing in Medicine," *America*, August 31, 1996, pp. 17–23.

9. "Talking to God: An Intimate Look at the Way We Pray," *Newsweek*, January 6, 1992, pp. 38–42; Larson and Larson, p. 136.

10. "Why We Pray," *Life*, March 1994, p. 62.

11. Findings summarized in Larson and Larson, pp. 137–139.

12. Herbert Benson, with Miriam Z. Klipper, *The Relaxation Response* (New York: Anchor, 1975), pp. 87–103, 141–154.

13. Benson, *Timeless Healing*, pp. 146–147.

14. Benson, *Timeless Healing*, pp. 134–137, 152.

15. Marty Kaplan, "Ambushed by Spirituality," *Time*, June 24, 1996, p. 62.

16. Benson, *Timeless Healing*, pp. 20–21.

17. Benson, *Timeless Healing*, pp. 30–64.

18. Benson, *Timeless Healing*, p. 203.

19. Benson, *Timeless Healing*, p. 155.

20. Benson, *Timeless Healing*, p. 211.

21. Findings summarized in Dale A. Matthews, David B. Larson, and Constance P. Barry, *The Faith Factor: An Annotated Bibliography of Clinical Research on Spiritual Subjects,* Rockville, MD: National Institute for Healthcare Research, 1993, p. 52.

22. Matthews, Larson, and Barry, p. 172.

23. Larson and Larson, pp. 141–143; cf. discussion in Larry Dossey, *Healing Words* (New York: HarperSanFrancisco, 1993), pp. 179–186.

24. Wallis, "Faith and Healing," p. 62.

25. Bible quotations are from the text of the New American Standard Bible, unless otherwise noted.

26. For an account of this conference, see Culligan, "Spirituality and Healing in Medicine," pp. 17–23.

27. Information on the OAM's activities can be found at the National Institutes of Health web site, *www.nih.gov.*

28. Wallis, "Faith and Healing," p. 62.

29. Elisabeth Kübler-Ross, *On Death and Dying* (New York: Macmillan, 1971).

30. Elisabeth Kübler-Ross, foreword to Raymond A. Moody, *Life After Life* (New York: Bantam, 1988; originally published in 1975).

31. Daniel Redwood, "Elisabeth Kübler-Ross 'On Death and Dying'"; 1995 interview of Kübler-Ross; text available at *www.doubleclickd.com/kubler.html.* See also Elisabeth Kübler-Ross, *On Life After Death* (Berkeley: Celestial Arts, 1991), pp. 43–44.

32. Moody, *Life After Life.*

Chapter 4

1. Raymond A. Moody, Jr., *Life After Life*, foreword Elisabeth Kübler-Ross (New York: Bantam, 1976; originally published 1975).

2. Michael B. Sabom, *Recollections of Death: A Medical Investigation* (New York: Harper & Row, 1982), pp. 1–13.

3. Sabom, p. 3.

4. Sabom, p. 2.

5. Sabom, p. 4.

6. Sabom, pp. 6–7.

7. Sabom, pp. 204–205.

8. Kenneth Ring, *Life at Death: A Scientific Investigation of the Near-Death Experience* (New York: Coward, McCann & Geoghegan, 1980).

9. Sabom, pp. 86–87.

10. Sabom, p. 64.

11. Sabom, pp. 65–66.

12. Sabom, p. 68.

13. Sabom, pp. 96–97.

14. Sabom, pp. 100–103.

15. Sabom, p. 104.

16. Sabom, pp. 69–72.

17. Sabom, pp. 111–113.

18. Susan Blackmore, *Dying to Live* (Buffalo, NY: Prometheus, 1993), pp. 122–125.

19. Sabom, pp. 84–86.

20. Blackmore, *Dying to Live,* p. 118.

21. Blackmore, *Dying to Live,* p. 119.

22. Sabom, pp. 104–105.

23. Susan Blackmore, *In Search of the Light* (Amherst, NY: Prometheus, 1996), pp. 239–245, 269–270.

24. Such anecdotal accounts run throughout the literature. For some additional well-documented examples, see Kenneth Ring and Madelaine Lawrence, "Further Evidence for Veridical Perception During Near-Death Experiences," *Journal of Near-Death Studies* 11, no. 4 (Summer 1993): 223–229.

25. Elisabeth Kübler-Ross, *On Children and Death* (New York: Collier, 1983), pp. 210–211.

26. Melvin Morse, with Paul Perry, *Closer to the Light: Learning from the Near-Death Experiences of Children* (New York: Ivy Books, 1990), pp. 1–8.

27. Morse, *Closer to the Light,* p. 30.

28. Peter Fenwick and Elizabeth Fenwick, *The Truth in the Light* (New York: Berkeley, 1995), pp. 45–46.

29. Blackmore, *Dying to Live*, pp. 49–53.

30. Fenwick and Fenwick, p. 214.

31. Fenwick and Fenwick, pp. 211–212.

32. Fenwick and Fenwick, p. 213.

33. Fenwick and Fenwick, pp. 116–118.

34. Ronald K. Siegel, "The Psychology of Life After Death," in Bruce Greyson and Charles P. Flynn, eds., *The Near-Death Experience* (Springfield, IL: Thomas, 1984), pp. 78–120.

35. Karlis Osis and Erlendur Haraldsson, *At the Hour of Death* (New York: Avon, 1977), provided an extensive cross-cultural survey of near-death apparitions and experiences in the United States and India and found similar patterns.

36. See Melvin Morse, with Paul Perry, *Transformed by the Light* (New York: Ballantine, 1992), and Kenneth Ring, *Heading Toward Omega* (New York: Morrow, 1985).

37. Fenwick and Fenwick, p. 118.

38. Carl Sagan, *Broca's Brain* (New York: Random House, 1979), pp. 301–311; cf. Carl Sagan, "The Amniotic Universe," and Carl B. Becker, "Why Birth Models Cannot Explain Near-Death Phenomena," in Greyson and Flynn, *The Near-Death Experience*, pp. 140–162.

39. Fenwick and Fenwick, pp. 217–218.

40. Quoted in Fenwick and Fenwick, p. 215.

41. Fenwick and Fenwick, pp. 218–221.

42. Michael A. Persinger, "Near Death Experiences: Determining the Neuroanatomical Pathways by Experiential Patterns and Simulation in Experimental Settings," in Luc Bessette, ed., *Le Processus de Guérison: Par-Delà la Souffrance ou la Mort/Healing: Beyond Suffering or Death* (Beauport, Québec, Canada: Publications MNH, 1994), pp. 284–285.

43. See M. A. Persinger, "Vectorial Cerebral Hemisphericity as Differential Sources for the Sensed Presence, Mystical Experiences and Religious Conversions," *Perceptual and Motor Skills* 76 (1993): 915–930.

44. Fenwick and Fenwick, p. 221.

45. See Melvin L. Morse, David Venecia, and Jerrold Milstein, "Near-Death Experiences: A Neurophysiologic Explanatory Model," *Journal of Near-Death Studies* 8, no. 1 (Fall 1989): 45–53.

46. "Scientific Evidence for Life After Death?" *Christianity Today*, August 27, 1976, p. 21.

47. Robert M. Herhold, "Kübler-Ross and Life After Death," *The Christian Century*, April 14, 1976, p. 363.

48. See Bruce Greyson and Nancy Evans Bush, "Distressing Near-Death Experiences," *Psychiatry* 55 (February 1992): 95–110; cf. P. M. H. Atwater, *Beyond the Light* (New York: Carol, 1994), pp. 27–45.

49. Maurice Rawlings, *Beyond Death's Door* (New York: Bantam, 1979), pp. 4–8.

50. Rawlings had a patient who became a committed Christian after such a hellish experience, even though he had no memory of the hellish aspect of it (Rawlings was attending the man as he was fading in and out of the experience and screaming "I am in hell!"). See Rawlings, *Beyond Death's Door*, p. 5; cf. Raymond A. Moody, Jr., with Paul Perry, *The Light Beyond*, foreword Andrew Greeley (New York: Bantam, 1989), pp. 151–152, and Atwater, p. 45.

51. George G. Ritchie, *Return from Tomorrow* (Waco, TX: Chosen Books, 1978), pp. 56–57.

52. Moody, *Life After Life*, pp. 65–67.

53. Raymond A. Moody, Jr., *Reflections on Life After Life* (New York: Bantam, 1978), pp. 34–35. Italics in original.

54. Ritchie, pp. 49, 53.

55. Ritchie, pp. 48–49, 55.

56. See Ring, *Life at Death*, pp. 165–167; cf. Moody, *The Light Beyond*, p. 49.

57. Elisabeth Kübler-Ross, *On Life After Death* (Berkeley: Celestial Arts, 1991), pp. 16, 60.

58. See Satwant Pasricha and Ian Stevenson, "Near-Death Experiences in India: A Preliminary Report," *The Journal of Nervous and Mental Disease* 174, no. 3 (1986): 165–170.

59. John C. Gibbs, "Moody's Versus Siegel's Interpretation of the Near-Death Experience: An Evaluation Based on Recent Research," *Anabiosis—The Journal of Near-Death Studies* 5, no. 2 (1985): 68. Cf. Sabom, pp. 56–57 and Ring, *Life at Death*, pp. 33–35.

60. George Gallup, Jr., *Adventures in Immortality* (New York: McGraw-Hill, 1982), pp. 198–201.

61. A historical survey of near-death-type visions is to be found in Carol Zaleski, *Otherworld Journeys* (New York: Oxford University Press, 1987); see also Barbara A. Walker and William J. Serdahely, "Historical Perspectives on Near-Death Phenomena," *Journal of Near-Death Studies* 9, no. 2 (Winter 1990): 105–121.

62. See Osis and Haraldsson.

63. Daniel Redwood, "Raymond Moody, M.D., Ph.D. 'Life After Life,' " interview posted on World Wide Web at *www.doubleclickd.com/raymoody.html*.

Chapter 5

1. The phrase, originally from Friedrich Schiller, was used frequently by the sociologist Max Weber. See H. H. Gerth and C. Wright Mills, eds., *From Max Weber: Essays in Sociology* (New York: Oxford University Press, 1946), pp. 51, 155.

2. See Friedrich Nietzsche, *Twilight of the Idols; The Anti-Christ*, tr. R. J. Hollingdale (Harmondsworth, Middlesex, England: Penguin, 1972); Friedrich Nietzsche, *Beyond Good and Evil*, tr. Walter Kaufmann (New York: Vintage, 1966), especially sections 257 and following.

3. See, for example, Hajo Holborn, *A History of Modern Germany* (Princeton: Princeton University Press, 1969), pp. 397–399; cf. Werner J. Dannhauser, "Friedrich Nietzsche," in Leo Strauss and Joseph Cropsey, eds., *History of Political Philosophy*, 2nd ed. (Chicago: Rand McNally, 1972), pp. 819–820.

4. As early as 1929, Heidegger wrote to a high official of the Ministry of Education complaining of the "growing Judaisation" of German university life. There is evidence that he had an unfavorable impact on the careers of three students and colleagues—a Jew, a Catholic, and a pacifist—because he saw them as insufficiently supportive of the Nazi regime. See Elzbieta Ettinger, *Hannah Arendt/Martin Heidegger* (New Haven: Yale University Press, 1995) pp. 36–37, 52–56. Günther Neske and Emil Kettering, *Martin Heidegger and National Socialism: Questions and Answers*, intr. Karsten Harries, tr. Lisa Harries (New York: Paragon House, 1990), provides an authoritative collection of documents relating to the later controversy among philosophers and intellectuals over Heidegger's Nazi involvement. A small collection of Heidegger's pro-Nazi speeches and

writings and other documents from the era is to be found in Martin Heidegger, *German Existentialism*, tr. Dagobert D. Runes (New York: Wisdom Library, 1965).

5. Richard Rorty, *Contingency, Irony, and Solidarity* (Cambridge: Cambridge University Press, 1989), p. 189.

6. Rorty, *Contingency*, p. xv.

7. Rorty, *Contingency*, p. 196

8. Rorty, *Contingency*, p. 192.

9. Rorty, *Contingency*, p. 198.

10. Heidegger let this phrase from a 1935 lecture stand when the lecture was published in 1953—much to the consternation of philosophical colleagues. Martin Heidegger, *An Introduction to Metaphysics*, tr. Ralph Manheim (New Haven: Yale University Press, 1959), p. 199. See Neske and Kettering, pp. xv–xvi. For the Nietzsche point, see Nietzsche, *Beyond Good and Evil*, section 260.

11. Rorty, *Contingency*, p. 194.

12. Rorty, *Contingency*, pp.163–164.

13. Biblical quotations are from the New American Standard Bible, unless otherwise noted.

14. Ancient sources estimated the number of Athenians executed by the Thirty Tyrants at 1,500. Simon Hornblower and Anthony Spawforth, *The Oxford Classical Dictionary*, 3rd edition (New York: Oxford University Press, 1996), p. 1513. See the texts of *The Clouds* and *The Apology of Socrates* in Thomas G. West and Grace Starry West, eds., *Four Texts on Socrates* (Ithaca: Cornell University Press, 1984), esp. pp. 84–85. See also Christopher Bruell, "Xenophon," in Leo Strauss and Joseph Cropsey, eds. *History of Political Philosophy*, 3rd ed. (Chicago: University of Chicago Press, 1987), pp. 103–107. As mentioned

in the Introduction, in the twentieth century, Leo Strauss tried to revise this Platonic/Socratic distinction between "esoteric" atheism and "exoteric" virtue. See Introduction, notes 6 and 10–11.

15. Richard Rorty, "Postmodernist Bourgeois Liberalism," in Thomas Docherty, ed., *Postmodernism* (New York: Columbia University Press, 1993), p. 325.

16. Martin Buber, *I and Thou*, tr. Walter Kaufmann (New York: Scribner's, 1970), p. 111.

17. Buber, pp. 109–110.

18. Buber, p. 115 (emphasis added).

19. Fred Hoyle, *The Origin of the Universe and the Origin of Religion* (Wakefield, RI: Moyer Bell, 1993), pp. 19–22.

20. Jerome Neyrey, ed., *The Social World of Luke-Acts* (Peabody, MA: Hendrickson, 1991), pp. 221–222. Cf. Spencer Perkins and Chris Rice, *More Than Equals: Racial Healing for the Sake of the Gospel* (Downers Grove, IL: InterVarsity Press, 1993), pp. 152–164.

21. See also Marcus C. Borg, *Jesus: A New Vision* (New York: HarperSanFrancisco, 1987), pp. 134–135.

22. Cf. Neyrey, pp. 316–317.

23. As the reference in Acts to "Jews and proselytes" implies, Judaism had already succeeded in attracting converts among other peoples in the ancient world—a tribute to the coherence and moral appeal of Jewish monotheism, especially when one considered the requirements for conversion, which included an insistence on "identification with the national aspiration of Jews"—that is, a shift in political and ethnic allegiance—as well as (for males) circumcision. See Louis H. Feldman, *Jew and Gentile in the Ancient World* (Princeton: Princeton University

Press, 1993), p. 288. In Christianity, however, the drive toward universalization became central. With it came a radical innovation: the separation of religion from national or tribal identity.

24. Alan F. Segal, *Paul the Convert* (New Haven: Yale University Press, 1990), p. xvi.

25. Text from New King James Version.

26. Hornblower and Spawforth, p. 411.

27. *Nichomachean Ethics,* 1123a–1124a. The edition used here is Aristotle, *Nichomachean Ethics,* tr. Martin Oswald (Indianapolis: Bobbs-Merrill, 1962).

28. Richard McKeon translates Aristotle's notion of "big-souledness" simply as "pride." See Richard McKeon, ed., *The Basic Works of Aristotle* (New York: Random House, 1941), p. 992.

29. As Nietzsche wrote, "Goal: the sanctification of the most powerful, most fertile and most excellently infamous forces, to use the old image: the deification of the devil." Quoted in Liliane Frey-Rohn, *Friedrich Nietzsche: A Psychological Approach to His Life and Work,* tr. Gary Massey (Zürich: Daimon, 1989), p. 191.

30. Nietzsche, *Beyond Good and Evil,* section 260. Cf. Friedrich Nietzsche, *On the Genealogy of Morals,* tr. Douglas Smith (Oxford: Oxford University Press, 1996), First Essay, sections 10–16, pp. 22–36.

31. Robert Ellsberg, ed., *Gandhi on Christianity* (Maryknoll, NY: Orbis, 1991), p. 12.

32. Ellsberg, p. 19.

33. E. Glenn Hinson, *The Early Church* (Nashville: Abingdon, 1996), p. 61.

34. Hinson, pp. 64–65. Cf., for example, R. R. Palmer and Joel Colton, *A History of the Modern World to 1815,* 4th ed. (New York: Knopf, 1971), p. 13.

35. Ellsberg, pp. 25–26.

36. See Nikolai Tolstoy, *Stalin's Secret War* (New York: Holt, Rinehart, and Winston, 1982).

37. See Klaus P. Fischer, *Nazi Germany: A New History* (New York: Continuum, 1997), pp. 130–131.

38. Fischer, pp. 359–363.

39. Quoted in Richard Grunberger, *The 12-Year Reich: A Social History of Nazi Germany 1933–1945* (New York: De Capo, 1997; originally published 1971), p. 442. Horst Wessel was a member of the Nazi SA who was shot in 1930 by a Communist, the pimp of the prostitute with whom Wessel had become infatuated and run off. The propaganda machine transformed him into a Nazi martyr. See Fischer, p. 225.

40. J. S. Conway, *The Nazi Persecution of the Churches 1933–45* (New York: Basic Books, 1968), p. 155.

41. Grunberger, p. 445.

42. Fischer, p. 38; cf. Nicholas Goodrick-Clarke, *The Occult Roots of Nazism: Secret Aryan Cults and Their Influence on Nazi Ideology*, foreword Rohan Bulter (New York: New York University Press, 1992).

43. For a description, see Robert Wuthnow, *The Restructuring of American Religion* (Princeton: Princeton University Press, 1988), pp. 244–250.

44. Thomas G. West, Jr., *The Politics of Revelation and Reason: Religion and Civic Life in the New Nations* (Lawrence, KS: University Press of Kansas, 1996), pp. 1–78.

45. Ellis Sandoz, *A Government of Laws: Political Theory, Religion, and the American Founding* (Baton Rouge: Louisiana State University Press, 1990), pp. 136–141.

46. On Franklin's belief, see Sandoz, p. 116; on Washington's belief, see West, *The Politics of Revelation and Reason*, p. 36.

47. Edmund Burke, *Reflections on the Revolution in France*, ed. Conor Cruise O'Brien (Baltimore: Penguin, 1969), pp. 186–188, 171–172.

48. See, for example, David Pryce-Jones, *The Strange Death of the Soviet Empire* (New York: Holt, 1995), pp. 29–35.

49. Quoted in Niels Nielsen, *Revolutions in Eastern Europe: Religious Roots* (Maryknoll, NY: Orbis, 1991), p. 155.

50. Mikhail Gorbachev, *Perestroika: New Thinking for Our Country and the World* (New York: Harper & Row, 1987), pp. 25–26.

51. "The Education of Mikhail Gorbachev," *Time*, January 4, 1988, pp. 18–30.

52. Aleksandr I. Solzhenitsyn, *The Mortal Danger*, tr. Michael Nicholson and Alexis Klimoff (New York: Harper & Row, 1980), pp. 32–34.

53. Henry S. Rowen and Charles Wolf, Jr., eds., *The Future of the Soviet Empire*, foreword Donald H. Rumsfeld (New York: St. Martin's, 1987).

54. George Weigel, *The Final Revolution: The Resistance Church and the Collapse of Communism* (New York: Oxford University Press, 1992).

55. See also Guenter Lewy, *Why America Needs Religion* (Grand Rapids, MI: Eerdman's, 1996), pp. 32–35, 46–47, 104–107.

56. "Is God Dead?" *Time*, April 8, 1966.

57. Nena and George O'Neill, *Open Marriage* (New York: Avon, 1972), p. 20.

58. Richard Cohen, "Open Marriage, Fidelity: Is an Old Era Dawning?" *The Washington Post*, October 11, 1977; Nena O'Neill, *The Marriage Premise* (New York: M. Evans, 1977); cf. Maxine Abrams, "Love, Sex, and Marriage: Past, Present, and Future," *Ladies Home Journal*, January 1984, p. 68.

59. Bertrand Russell, *Religion and Science* (Oxford: Oxford University Press, 1961; originally published 1935), p. 13.

60. Thomas Kuhn, *The Structure of Scientific Revolutions*, 2nd ed. (Chicago: University of Chicago Press, 1970).

61. For a readable summary, see Paul Davies and John Gribben, *The Matter Myth* (New York: Simon & Schuster, 1992), pp. 221–224.

62. Cf. Buber: "The economy as the house of the will to profit and the state as the house of the will to power participate in life as long as they participate in the spirit. If they abjure the spirit, they abjure life." Buber, *I and Thou*, p. 98.

63. Sigmund Freud, *The Future of an Illusion*, tr. James Strachey, intr. Peter Gay (New York: Norton, 1989), p. 69.

64. See Hans Küng, *Global Responsibility: The Search for a New World Ethic* (New York: Crossroad, 1991).

65. Hans Küng and Karl-Josef Kuschel, eds., *A Global Ethic: The Declaration of the Parliament of the World's Religions* (New York: Continuum, 1993).

Index

acceptance (virtue), 92–93

accident, as explanation for human existence and cosmic order, 5, 7, 23–24, 52–53, 89, 140. *See also* contingency, coincidences

Acts of the Apostles, 152–53, 157

adultery, 75, 144, 164

afterlife, 1–2, 6, 15, 17–18, 55, 75, 100–101, 129–130. *See also* near-death experience
opinion polling on belief in 1, 135

agape. See love

agnostic (term), 37

agnosticism, 1–2, 5, 20, 36–37, 53, 58, 62, 64, 69, 77, 82–83, 85, 92, 124

AIDS, use of meditation in treatment of, 85

Alcibiades, 144

alcohol abuse, 76
divorce and risk of, 67
religious belief and levels of, 61, 64, 75, 81
as symptom of demoralization in Soviet collapse, 162–63

Alcoholics Anonymous, 69, 76

Allen, Woody, 68–69

American Association of Christian Counselors, 72

American founding, religious influences in, 159–61

American Psychiatric Association, 58

American Psychological Association, 10, 58

American Revolution, 159–61

Andrews, Lewis, 72

anthropic principle, 7–9, 10, 11,
    18, 21–55
  defined, 22–23
  proposed, 21–22

anthropic reasoning, 30, 179 n. 53

anthropocentrism, 43

Antichrist, 140

Antioch (New Testament), 153

Aristophanes, 144

Aristotle, 13, 32–33, 154–55

Arnold, Matthew, 4

Aryan movement, 159

atheism, 1, 3, 5–6, 10, 12–13,
    18–20, 23–24, 34, 36–37,
    44, 53, 57–59, 62–63,
    64, 76–77, 82–83, 87,
    88–89, 92
  ancient philosophers and, 5–6,
    44, 144–145, 171–72 n. 6,
    172–73 n. 10–11
  modern philosophers and,
    5–6, 33–37, 44, 144
  modern psychology and, 10, 24,
    57–78
  social catastrophe and,
    159–64

Athens (ancient), 144

atom, primeval, 26–27, 41. See also
    Lemaître, Georges

atomic bomb, 27

Augustine, 35, 40, 176–78 n. 33

Auschwitz, 69, 141

autoscopic perception, 10, 104,
    106, 113, 119, 121. See also
    near-death experience
  defined, 104

baby universes, 8, 49, 51–53

Balkans, 168

behaviorist school (psychology), 58

Being of Light (near-death experi-
    ences), 9, 100, 102, 130,
    131–33

belief in God. See faith; God

Bell Laboratories, 27

Benson, Herbert, 80, 84–88, 94, 96

Bible 3–4, 34, 36, 73, 92, 130,
    135, 150. See also Hebrew
    Bible; New Testament;
    Genesis, Book of

big bang theory, 7, 26–28, 31, 51
  origin of term, 27

biology, 30, 34, 47–48, 85, 87–88,
    140, 148, 156, 167. See also
    Darwin, Charles

black hole, 51–53

Blackmore, Susan, 113–117, 119, 121

blood pressure
  meditation and levels of, 84–85, 89
  religious belief and levels of, 81

Bolt, Robert, 15

bomb, atomic. See atomic bomb

Brief History of Time,
    A (Hawking), 42

bubble universes, 8, 49, 53

Buber, Martin, 14–16,
146–148
Buddhism, 75, 92, 116, 169
Burke, Edmund, 160
Byrd, Randolph, 90–91

Cambridge University, 5, 22
cancer, meditation and treatment
of, 85
Capital (Marx), 37
caprice, in postmodern
philosophy, 146
carbon, and anthropic principle,
29–30
cardiac arrhythmia, meditation and
treatment of, 85
Carter, Brandon, 7, 22–25, 28–29
catastrophism, 34–35
Catholic Church. *See* Roman
Catholic Church
cause, efficient, 32–33
cause, final, 32–33
cause, first (deism), 33
Chamberlain, Neville, 16
chance. *See* accident
Chesterton, Gilbert K., 149
Christ, 153, 164. *See also* Jesus
in near-death experiences, 9,
100–01, 103, 118, 129–30,
133–34
Christian Century, The, 129
Christian counseling. *See*
psychology

Christianity Today, 128
Christianity, 4, 75, 142–43, 149,
169
early history of, 149–53
historical failings of, 149–50,
152, 156–57
as "imperial religion," 157
as moral revolution, 154–55
as multiethnic religion, 142,
149–56
Church. *See* Roman Catholic
Church
church attendance
blood pressure, lower, and, 81
cirrhosis of the liver, reduced
risk for, and, 80
divorce, reduced risk for, and, 64
drug abuse, reduced risk for,
and, 64
good health and, 81
heart disease, reduced risk for,
and, 80
psychological well-being and,
82–83
marital satisfaction and, 64
suicide, reduced risk for, and, 63
churches. *See* Christianity
Churchill, Winston, 16
cirrhosis of the liver, religious
belief and levels or risks of, 81
citizenship, Roman, 154
Classical and Quantum Gravity, 52
Clouds, The (Aristophanes), 144

coincidences
  anthropic, 7–8, 22–25, 28–30,
    31, 39, 42–43, 48, 50
  large number, 22, 24–25
Columbus, Christopher, 54
Comedy of Errors, The
  (Shakespeare), 45
Communism, 13, 158
  collapse of Soviet, 161–63
compassion, 133, 142, 154.
  See also love
congregation-based counseling.
  See psychology
conscience, 15–16, 142, 168
constants, fundamental, 22, 24,
  28, 39, 43, 53
contingency, 52–53, 140–41. *See*
  also accident
Contingency, Irony, and Solidarity
  (Rorty), 141
Copernicanism, 4, 22–26, 32–33
Copernicus, Nicolaus, 4, 21–23,
  25–26, 32, 38
Cornelius (New Testament
  story), 153
cosmic background
  radiation, 27
cosmology, 7–8, 18, 22–55, 148.
  See also big bang theory,
  anthropic principle
Cox, Harvey, 3
Creationists, 34
Critias, 145

Critique of Judgment (Kant), 46–47
Croats, 151
crucifixion, 150, 154
culture
  American, 3, 60
  conflicts or differences in, 142,
    151, 147
  Nazism and German, 140
  near-death experiences and, 123,
    136
  postsecularism and contempo-
    rary, 140
  reason and, 158
  religion and, 150–155, 157
  secularism and modern, 1–3,
    23–24, 60, 96, 158

Darwin, Charles, 2–4, 7, 23, 26,
  35–37, 46–48, 52–53, 57–58
Davies, Paul, 50, 54
Dawkins, Richard, 47
"death of God." *See* God, "death of."
Declaration of Independence, 160
defibrillator, operation of observed
  in near-death experiences,
  106, 108–12, 114–16
deism, 33, 160
  in American founding, 160
delinquency, juvenile. *See* juvenile
  delinquency
democracy
  Athenian, 145
  modern liberal, 13, 166

Dennett, Daniel, 47

depression (psychological), religious belief and reduced levels of, 61, 64, 73

Descartes, René, 33, 145

design (of universe), 7–10, 19, 23, 26, 40–41, 50, 54, 74, 76, 80, 88

Dicke, Robert, 24

Diderot, Denis, 34, 44

Dirac, Paul, 25

"disenchantment of the world," 139

divorce rates, 59, 61, 63

divorce
changing sexual mores and rising rates of, 59, 163
public health consequences of, 67, 163–64
religious belief and lowered levels of, 61, 64
religious prohibitions on, 67, 164

dogmatism
reason or science and, 20, 158, 164–65, 167–68
religion and, 158, 164–65, 168

Doherty William, 68

drug abuse
meditation and levels of, 84
religious belief and levels of, 61, 63, 66, 75–76, 89

Eddington, Arthur, 25, 44

Egyptian Book of the Dead, 135

Einstein, Albert, 165

electromagnetism, and anthropic coincidences, 8, 24, 28–30, 39

Eliot, George, 36

Ellis, Albert, 58

Enlightenment, 33–34, 63, 139, 156–161, 166–67

Epicureans, 44

esotericism, 12–13, 144, 171–72 n. 6, 172–173 n. 9–11

Everett, Hugh, 49–51

evil
discernment of, 167–69
Nazism as religion of, 158–59
origin and nature of, 144
"problem of," 55, 75–76
reason and, 143–45, 167
reckoning for in afterlife, 129–30

evolution. *See also* anthropic principle; big bang theory; cosmology; Darwin, Charles; Darwinism
biological, 2, 7, 26, 28, 47–48, 87–89, 137
of universe, 7–8, 25, 26, 28–31

existentialism, 24

explanatory style, 73

faith, 2, 3, 11–12, 26, 53–55, 74, 76, 164
  as "illusion" or "neurosis," 57
  health and, 60–65, 72, 74, 77, 79–82, 86–88, 95
  "loss of," 4, 33–36
  reason and, 139–69
  reason and in Pascal's Wager, 76–77
"faith factor," 62, 95
Farrow, Mia, 68
Fenwick, Peter, 120–122, 124, 127
Feuerbach, Ludwig, 36, 59
Final Revolution, The (Weigel), 163
fine-tuning (of universe), 8, 22, 29, 31, 52. *See also* design (of universe); anthropic principle
flatness problem (cosmology), 39
forgiveness, psychology and, 70–71
Framers, American, 159–60, 166
Frankl, Viktor, 69–70
Franklin, Benjamin, 160
French Revolution, 159–60
Freud, Sigmund, 10, 24, 37, 57–62, 66, 69–72, 78, 82, 88–89, 167
  critique of methods of, 62, 182 n. 16, 183 n. 21
  influence of, 59–63
  science and, 58–63, 78, 167

theories as substitute religion, 59, 62
  theories on religion, 57–60, 62–63, 69–72, 78, 82, 88–89, 167
  theories on sexuality, 59, 66
  theory of dammed-up libido, 66
Fromm, Erich, 69
fundamental constants. *See* constants, fundamental
Future of an Illusion, The (Freud), 57, 167

Gaia theory, 51–52, 54
Galileo Galilei, 32–33, 35, 38, 41
Gallup Poll, 64–65, 83
  and near-death experiences, 135
Gamow, George, 27
Gandhi, Mahatma, 156–57
Gay, Peter, 59
Genesis, Book of, 3–4, 26, 52
Gentiles (New Testament), 152–53
Glynn, Gabriele, 16–17, 19, 135
God. *See also* faith; prayer; religion
  belief in among physicians, 82
  belief in among psychiatrists, 58
  belief in among psychologists, 10, 58
  culture and human understanding of, 150–56

"death of," 3–6, 13, 26, 37, 139–40, 145, 147, 163
opposition to and social catastrophe, 159–64
remergence of in postmodern culture, 139–40, 150, 161–65
survey data on belief in, 1, 10, 58, 82
God hypothesis, 53–54
Good Samaritan (New Testament Parable), 151
Gorbachev, Mikhail, 162–63
Gospel. *See* New Testament
Gould, Stephen Jay, 47–48
Graham, Billy, 73
gravity, anthropic principle and, 8, 24, 28–29
unified theory and, 39
Greek philosophers.
    See philosophy, ancient
Greeks (New Testament era), 152–53
Gribbin, John, 50–52, 54
Groundhog Day (film), 46
Gypsies, 159

Hamlet (Shakespeare), 6
happiness
    prayer and, 83–84
    religious belief and, 61–62, 64–65, 67, 72, 73–77
Hartle, Jim, 41–42
Harvard Medical School, 65, 80, 84, 94

Harvard University, 2–3, 5, 30, 47, 65, 80, 84–85, 94
Hawking, Stephen W., 21–22, 40–42, 51, 54
health
    religious belief and mental, 11, 20, 61–65, 72–77. *See also* prayer; meditation
    religious belief and physical, 11, 20, 61, 80–82, 85–89
heart disease, religious belief and levels of, 80–81, 89
Hebrew Bible, 92, 150
Heidegger, Martin, 12, 140–41, 143
hell, 100, 129, 130
    hellish near-death experience, 129
Henderson, Lawrence, 30
Henry VIII, 15
Hinduism, 92, 157, 169
    near-death experiences of Hindus, 129, 134
Hitler, Adolf, 12, 159
Hobbes, Thomas, 62, 149
Holbach, Baron d', 34
Holy Spirit, 152–53
honor, 13, 15–16
hope, 74–75, 86, 88, 162
Hoyle, Fred, 27, 30–31, 54, 148, 179 n. 53
Hubble, Edwin, 27
Hume, David, 34, 44
Huxley, Thomas H., 37, 53

I-It. *See* Buber, Martin

illusion, religious belief as,
10, 57, 71–74, 77, 88–89.
See also Freud, Sigmund

In Memoriam (Tennyson), 35

In the Beginning (Gribbin), 52

inferiority complex, 59

infertility, meditation and treatment of, 85, 89

inflation theory (cosmology), 39, 51, 53

Inquisition, 158

insomnia, meditation and treatment of, 85

International Association of Near-Death Studies, 120

International Astronomical Union, 7

Ireland, Northern, 168

Isaiah, 92, 150

Islam, 92, 158, 169

I-You. *See* Buber, Martin

Jefferson, Thomas, 160

Jehovah's Witnesses, 159

Jesus, 17, 67, 118, 130,
133–34, 144, 147, 150–51,
153, 155, 157–59, 166, 168.
See also Christ
attitude to women, 151–52
quoted, 93, 133, 144,
151, 155, 168

Jews. *See also* Judaism
Christian persecution of, 158

Nazi persecution of and
genocide against, 12–14, 140,
159, 195 n. 10
of first-century Palestine,
150–153, 196–97 n. 23

Joplin, Janis, 84

Joshua, 150

Judaism, 75, 169.
See also Jews

Jung, Carl, 57, 69

juvenile delinquency, divorce
and, 67

Kant, Immanuel, 47

Kaplan, Marty, 85

Kübler-Ross, Elisabeth, 18,
96–97, 117–18, 134

Kuhn, Thomas, 47, 165

Küng, Hans, 169

large number coincidences. *See*
coincidences, large number

Larson, David B., 61, 80–81, 88,
95–96

Lemaître, Georges, 27

Lenin, Vladimir Ilyich, 162

Leslie, John, 30

leukemia, 90

Leviathan (Hobbes), 149

Life After Life (Moody), 9,
97, 99, 101

life review. *See* near-death
experience

Light. *See* Being of Light; near-
    death experience
logos. See reason
Lolita (Nabokov), 144, 146
love *(agape)*, 9, 14, 16–17, 36,
    69–71, 74, 100, 130–34, 147
Lovelock, James, 51
Lyell, Charles, 34–36

Mademoiselle, 60
magic, in contrast to religion, 90,
    92–94
Maimonides, Moses, 40
Man for All Seasons, A (Bolt), 15
Man's Search for Meaning
    (Frankl), 70
many histories. *See* many universes
many universes (cosmology),
    49–50
many worlds. *See* many universes
marital satisfaction, religious belief
    and, 61, 64
marriage, 14–16, 61, 64, 159, 164
Martha and Mary (New Testament
    story), 151
Marx, Karl, 3, 37, 165, 167
Marxism, 3, 24
Marxism-Leninism, 158, 162
Mary (mother of Jesus), 134
Maslow, Abraham, 70
materialism, 18, 38, 72, 77, 89,
    120, 146
    "death of," 38

mechanism (doctrine), 4–5, 18,
    23, 26, 31–38, 39–40, 43,
    46–47, 62, 89
medical education, religion and,
    95–96
medicine. *See* health
meditation, 80, 83–89, 93, 116.
    See also prayer
    as form of prayer, 83, 87, 93
    health benefits of, 80, 83–89
Meduna, L. J., 125–27
mental illness, increased risk
    for among nonbelievers,
    75. *See also* health; prayer;
    meditation
Middle Ages, 157–58
Miller, J. Hillis, 4, 36
mind-body connection,
    11, 95
modern culture. *See* culture
modern era, 1–7, 13, 18–20,
    21–24, 26, 32–38, 43–44, 46,
    54–55, 58, 60, 62–63, 69, 72,
    74–77, 88–89, 140–43, 145,
    147–49, 155, 156, 158–61,
    164, 166–67
    defined, 38
monkey and typewriter thesis,
    44–46
Moody, Raymond, 9–10, 18,
    97, 99–103, 128, 130, 131,
    135, 136
    quoted, 136–37

morality, 5–6, 11–13, 57, 60, 63,
    66–69, 72, 74–77, 129–30,
    134–35, 140–48, 154–56,
    161–63, 165–69
    public-private distinction and,
    5–6, 13–16, 143–45, 171–72
    n. 6, 172–73, n. 9–11
More, Thomas (saint), 15
Morse, Melvin, 18, 118–19, 128
Moses, 150
Murray, Bill (actor), 46

Nabokov, Vladimir, 144
National Institute for Healthcare
    Research, 80, 95
National Institutes of Health,
    61, 94
    Office of Alternative Medicine
    of, 94
National Library of
    Medicine, 18
National Opinion Research
    Center, 82
National Socialism. See Nazism
natural selection, 7, 26, 46–48, 52.
    See also biology; evolution;
    Darwin, Charles
Nazism, 12–13, 77, 140, 143,
    158–59
    as antireligion, 158–59
NDE. See near-death experience
near-death experience, 9–12, 18,
    20, 96–97, 99–137

among Hindus, 129, 134
    anoxia as proposed explanation
    for, 121–22, 128
    as possible hallucination, 9–10,
    18, 123, 128, 136–37
    auditory cues and, 113
    "autoscopic" perception and,
    10, 99, 102–20, 121, 136–37
    Being of Light in, 9, 100, 102,
    130, 131–33
    birth tunnel memory as pro-
    posed explanation for, 124
    children and, 117–19
    cross-cultural similarities of,
    118, 123, 134–36
    encounters with deceased rela-
    tives in, 9, 100, 103, 117–18,
    134, 135–36
    endorphins as proposed explana-
    tion for, 124–25
    figure of Christ in, 9, 100–01,
    103, 118, 129–30, 133–34
    hellish, 129–30
    historical examples of, 135
    hypercarbia as proposed explana-
    tion for, 125–27
    life review and, 9, 100, 102–03,
    130–33
    prevalence of, 103, 135
    proposed naturalistic explana-
    tions for, 113–16, 120–28
    right temporal lobe involvement
    in, 127

"theology" of, 130–35, 137
"transcendental," 103, 128, 135
tunnel and, 9, 100, 102–03,
    122, 124
neurosis, religion as, 10, 19, 57,
    61, 65, 71. *See also* Freud,
    Sigmund
neutrino, anthropic principle and,
    8, 31
neutron, anthropic principle and,
    29–30
New Age, 93–94
*New Harvard Guide to Psychiatry,
    The*, 65
New Left, 3
New Life (counseling clinics), 71
New Testament, 67, 69, 92, 130,
    133–34, 142–44, 147, 149,
    150–51, 155–56, 166, 168
New York Review of Books, 40
New York Times, 11, 59, 70–71
Newton, Isaac, 33
Nichomachean Ethics
    (Aristotle), 13
Nietzsche, Friedrich, 12, 37, 77,
    140–41, 143, 155
NIH. *See* National Institutes of
    Health
nihilism, 6, 12, 14, 16, 147
Noah, 34
no-boundary proposal, 41–42
Novak, Michael, 20
nuclear fission, 27

nuclear fusion, 27
nuclear strong force, anthropic
    principle and, 28–29
nuclear weak force, anthropic
    priciple and, 28–29
Nuremberg Party rally (1934), 159

OAM. *See* National Institutes of
    Health, Office of Alternative
    Medicine of
Oedipus complex, 59–60
Office of Alternative Medicine
    (NIH). *See* National Institutes
    of Health
Old Testament. *See*
    Hebrew Bible
On Death and Dying (Kübler-
    Ross), 96
O'Neill, George, 164
O'Neill, Nena, 164
Open Marriage (O'Neill and
    O'Neill), 164
optimism, 72–74
Origin of Species, The (Darwin),
    36–37
Orwell, George, 159–60
out-of-body experience, 10,
    104, 113, 116, 119,
    120–22, 128
    surgery and, 104
out-of-body like experience, 120,
    127. *See also* near-death expe-
    rience

oxygen, and anthropic principle, 28. *See also* near-death experience, anoxia as proposed explanation for

paradigm shift, 47, 140, 164–65
parallel universes, 8, 48–51
Parliament of the World's Religions, 169
Pascal, Blaise, 76–77
Pascal's Wager, 76–77
Paul (apostle), 12, 130, 151, 153
    quoted, 12, 130, 153
Peacocke, Arthur, 54
peak experiences. *See* Maslow, Abraham
Peck, M. Scott, 11, 70
Pendleton, B. F., 83
Penrose, Roger, 21
Penzias, Arno, 27
People of the Lie (Peck), 70
permissiveness, sexual. *See* sexuality
Persinger, Michael, 127
pessimism, 73
Peter (apostle), 152–53
Pfister, Oskar, 58–59
Phaedo (Plato), 6
Philip (evangelist), 153
philosophes, 34
philosophy, 1–2, 5–7, 12–13, 17–18, 20, 22–25, 31–38, 41, 43–48, 59, 76–77, 139–69.
    See also specific philosophers

ancient, 5–6, 12–13, 31–33, 144–145, 154–55
modern, 5–7, 12, 20, 22–25, 31–38, 41, 43–48, 76–77, 139, 140, 143, 145–46, 147–48, 149, 155, 156–61, 164, 167
postmodern, 38, 140–48
physicians, religious beliefs of, 82
physics. *See* anthropic principle; big bang theory; cosmology
placebo effect, 85–86
Plato, 6, 13
Platonism, 135
Polkinghorne, John, 54
Poloma, M. M., 83
Pope John Paul II, 41–42
popes, Catholic, 157–58
positivism, 24, 164–65
postmodernism. *See* philosophy, postmodern
postsecularism, 38, 53–54, 57, 72, 80, 82, 92, 94–96, 140, 148, 161
prayer, 17, 19, 76, 87, 160. *See also* meditation
    health benefits of, 80, 82, 84
    "intercessory," studies of effects of on disease, 90–92
    polling data on, 82–83, 95
    psychological benefits of, 83–84
    types of, 83
primeval atom, 26–27, 41

Principles of Geology (Lyell), 34, 36

private vs. public. *See* morality

problem of evil. *See* evil, problem of

problem of measurement (quantum mechanics), 49–50

Prodigal Son (New Testament parable), 147

promiscuity. *See* sexuality

proton, anthropic principle and, 30–31

Providence, belief of American founders in, 160

psychiatry, 10–11, 58, 60, 68–69, 70–71, 82, 167. *See also* Freud, Sigmund

psychoanalysis, 57–60, 68–69, 70–71. *See also* Freud, Sigmund

psychology. *See also* Freud, Sigmund

  Christian and congregation-based, 71–72

  postsecular trends and revival of religion in, 10–11, 57–78, 167

public vs. private. *See* morality

punctuated equilibrium (biology), 48

quantum mechanics, 38, 42, 48–49, 165

race riots, 74

random universe, 4–5, 7, 8, 18–19, 21–55, 57

randomness. *See* accident; contingency

rational-emotive therapy, 58

Rawlings, Maurice, 129

Reagan administration, 13

reason, 10–11, 15, 19–20, 37, 55, 76–77, 140, 149

  limitations of, 139–40, 143, 145–46, 148, 155, 156, 158, 164–65, 166–69

  prestige of, in modern era, 149

  revelation and, 41, 76–77, 146, 165, 166–69

  Spirit and, 146, 165, 166–69

red shift, 27

Redbook, 64

Reformation, 158

relaxation response, 84, 86. *See* meditation

Relaxation Response, The (Benson), 84

religion. *See also specific religions*

  commonalities among, 169

  Communist collapse and, 161–63

  decline of and social problems, 74

  Enlightenment and, 32–33, 158, 161

  evolutionary explanation for, 88

  health (physical) and, 79–87, 92

  magic versus, 92–93

  medical education and, 95–96

religion, *continued*
mental well-being and, 61–65,
67, 73–75, 77
near-death experiences and, 100,
128–29, 134, 136
optimism and, 73
philosophy and, 5–6, 20
predictions of demise
of, 139
psychology and, 10, 11, 19,
57–63, 167
rational foundation for apparently undermined, 4
resurgence in contemporary psychology, 69–72
revival among young, 66
science and, 2, 4, 8–9, 20, 23,
26, 32–38, 41–48, 53–55,
58–59, 62, 136, 149, 156,
159, 163, 165
tolerance about as lesson of
near-death experience, 134
traditional discredited among intellectuals, 2–4, 33–38, 139
tribalism of traditional,
149–58
Religion and Science (Russell),
23, 26
religious drive, 74, 80
Renaissance, 158
Republic (Plato), 135
revelation and reason, 166–69
in Pascal's Wager, 76–77

Revolution of Light (East
Germany), 161
Revolutionary war, 160
Rieff, Philip, 60
Ring, Kenneth, 103
Ritchie, George, 11, 130, 133
Road Less Traveled, The (Peck),
13, 70
Roman Catholic Church, 3,
33–34, 41, 157–58
early history of, 152–53, 156, 157
Roman Empire, 150, 154, 157
Rorty, Richard, 141–47
Royal College of Psychiatrists, 120
Russell, Bertrand, 5, 23–24, 26,
37, 53, 164
Russell, Robert John, 54

Sabom, Michael, 100–05, 108–09,
111–31, 115–16, 119,
122–23, 125–28, 135–36
afterlife beliefs of before near-
death investigation, 100–01
Sagan, Carl, 43, 124
Samaritans (first–century
Palestine), 151
San Francisco General Hospital, 90
Schrödinger, Erwin, 49,
science and religion. *See* religion,
science and
Secular City, The (Cox), 3
secularism, 2–3, 5, 8, 19, 38, 54,
63, 72, 77, 96, 139

secularization, 3, 57–58, 163–64.
   See also God, "death of"
self, in postmodern philosophy,
   142, 145–47
   deactualized (Buber), 15,
   146–47
self-discipline, 74
Seligman, Martin, 73
Serbs, 151
Sermon on the Mount, 155, 156
sex addiction, 76
sexuality
   Freud's theories and, 59, 66
   religious prohibitions on
      immorality, 75, 144, 164, 169
   satisfaction in marriage, 61, 64
   sexual revolution and conse-
      quences, 65–66, 163–64
Shakespeare, William, 6, 44–46
Shklar, Judith, 141
"Silent Night"
   (Christmas carol), 159
Silk, Joseph, 21
sin, 65, 75, 133, 150, 156, 168
Skinner, B. F., 58
Smolin, Lee, 51–54
smoothness problem
   (cosmology), 39
Socrates, 6, 144–45
Solidarity (Polish political movement), 161
solidarity, Richard Rorty's conception of, 142–43, 147

Solzhenitsyn, Aleksandr, 163
soul, 1–2, 6, 10, 20, 57,
   59, 62–63, 71, 74, 78,
   80, 82, 88, 93, 95, 97,
   116, 120, 136, 139, 149,
   154–55, 166
Soviet Union, 158, 161–63
Spirit and reason, 166–69
spiritual growth, 69, 71, 94
spirituality, 20, 92–93, 150, 157,
   161, 163
Spock, Benjamin, 60
SS (Nazi Germany), 12
steady state theory, 27, 30
Stein, Gertrude, 87
Strauss, Leo, 12–14, 171–72 n. 6,
   172–73 n. 9–11
stress, religious belief and reduced
   levels of, 61, 64, 79
suicide, religious belief and
   reduced risks of, 61, 63, 67,
   80, 89
surgery, religious belief and
   more rapid recovery from,
   61, 64
Swastika, 159

technology, 149
teleology, 31–33, 38, 46
Ten Commandments, 75
Tennyson, Alfred, 35–36
theism, 33, 43
theodicy. *See* evil, problem of

theology, 3, 8, 76, 169
near-death experience
and, 130
science and, 33, 42, 53, 54,
94, 165
theory of everything. *See* unified
theory
therapeutic, "triumph of." *See*
Rieff, Philip
Thirty Tyrants, 145
Tibetan Book of the Dead, 135
Time (magazine), 79, 88
"Is God Dead?" cover story, 3, 164
Time/CNN Poll, 95
tongues, miracle of (New
Testament), 152
transcendental meditation. *See*
meditation
tribalism
reason and, 158
religion and, 149–158, 166
Trilling, Lionel, 60

unbelief. *See* atheism
unified theory, 39–40, 43
universal conception of man (ancient Greek philosphers), 154
universal values, 140–41
universe, evolution of from big
bang. *See* evolution, of universe; anthropic principle; cosmology; design (of universe)

universe, random. *See* random
universe
Universes (Leslie), 30
universes. *See* many universes; baby
universes; bubble universes;
parallel universes
University of Freiburg, 140

Vatican Council II, 3
Vatican, 41
Vietnam War, 3, 74
virtue, classical philosophers' con-
ception of in contrast to
Christian, 154–55
Voltaire, 33

W., Bill (Bill Wilson), 76
Wagoner, Robert, 21
Ward, Keith, 42
Washington, George, 160
water, nature of as illustration of
anthropic principle, 29–30
Weigel, George, 163
Weinberg, Steven, 40
well-being. *See* happiness
Wessel, Horst, 159
Wheeler, John, 21, 24, 50
Will, George F., 15
Wilson, Robert W., 27

Yankelovich Partners, 95
young-earth theorists, 34